INNER GENIUS OUTER GURU

A HEART-CENTERED ENTREPRENEUR'S GUIDE TO
UNLIMITED POTENTIAL FOR GROWTH IN INCOME
AND FREEDOM IN LIFESTYLE WITHOUT BURNOUT

AVADHI DHRUV

Difference Press

Washington, DC, USA

Copyright © Avadhi Dhruv, 2022

All rights reserved. No part of this book may be reproduced in any form without permission in writing from the author. Reviewers may quote brief passages in reviews.

ISBN 978-1-68309-307-7

Published 2022

DISCLAIMERS

No part of this publication may be reproduced or transmitted in any form or by any means, mechanical or electronic, including photocopying or recording, or by any information storage and retrieval system, or transmitted by email without permission in writing from the author. Neither the author nor the publisher assumes any responsibility for errors, omissions, or contrary interpretations of the subject matter herein. Any perceived slight of any individual or organization is purely unintentional.

The information you obtain in this book is solely for informational purposes. It does not constitute nor is it meant to be legal, medical, financial, or other professional advice. The author does not make any warranties about the completeness, reliability, and accuracy of this information. Further, the scenarios presented may not be suitable for your particular situation. Any action you take upon the information provided is strictly at your own risk. You should consult with a licensed professional where appropriate. Neither the author nor the publisher will be liable for any losses and/or damages of any type in connection with this book.

The names and identifiers of the persons involved in the anecdotes presented have been changed for anonymity purposes. Any resemblance to any person, whether living or dead, is purely coincidental. Further, some anecdotes may be composites of other situations or experiences of the author.

Brand and product names are trademarks or registered trademarks of their respective owners.

Cover Design: Jennifer Stimson

Editing: Cory Hott

CONTENTS

1. Do You Deserve a Life of Abundance and Freedom? — 1
2. A True Story of Discovery – Why You Can Be Who You Wish to Be — 7
3. Walk the Abundance Path for Unlimited Growth — 23
4. Identify Your Top Three Business Goals This Year — 33
5. Connect with Your Inner Genius for Infinite Confidence — 55
6. Connect with Your Purpose – Your Dharma — 77
7. Be Yourself to Grow Your Audience — 87
8. Get Paid for Your Unique Value — 105
9. Shine Your Light — 119
10. Honor Your Value — 135
11. Ready to Create Sustainable Business Income? — 151
12. Transform the World through Your Business — 167

Appendix A: Affirmations — 185
Appendix B: Belief Statements — 187
Acknowledgments — 189
About the Author — 195
About Difference Press — 199
Other Books by Difference Press — 203
Gift for Readers — 205
Other Books by Avadhi — 207

To my mom, for your unconditional love, perseverance, and devotion to making a tremendous contribution in the world.

A mother's love is unmatched because it is unconditional and divine. I feel blessed to have a mother who exemplifies beauty inside and out.

The strength and courage you are, Mom, is extraordinary.

Thank you for being my inspiration. I love you to the starry galaxies and back!

"Entrepreneurship is not for the faint of heart. It requires tremendous sacrifice of your false self, so that your true self can shine. It demands the magnificence within you to show up fully."

— AVADHI DHRUV

1

DO YOU DESERVE A LIFE OF ABUNDANCE AND FREEDOM?

Having a sustainable income in business is difficult, and most young businesses fail within the first three years. Knowing which business is right for you can be quite confusing and overwhelming. If you have gotten the degrees, read the books, watched the webinars, and still don't know how to maintain a sustainable income without burning yourself out, you are not alone; there is a reason why you are stuck.

Lack of clarity on what kind of business to choose, and not knowing what priorities to focus on within your business in its early stages, are factors that alone can kill your business dreams before they take off.

HAVE AN ABUNDANT MINDSET FOR SUSTAINABLE BUSINESS INCOME

When you live in constant fear of running out of savings, without a clear idea of when or from where your next income will come, it can trap your mind in a scarcity mindset. A scarcity mindset sees limitations and constraints everywhere. When there seems to be no way out of this misery, dreams don't seem to be even a remote possibility, much less a strong probability.

The mental struggle also has its impacts on various other areas of your life – such as health, relationships, social life, sense of esteem, confidence, and success. Feeling like a constant failure is debilitating to say the least, and the continuous struggle can cause stress that can affect your relationships with your significant other and the people around you.

Not only that, but the biggest trouble is that you have no idea how to plan ahead. You hesitate to make plans or go on trips or vacations because, again, the lack of money and fear of running out of the finite amount of savings – not knowing how long you will need them to survive on – can completely confine you into a dark room with no ray of light coming through. The dark room of an unknown future, for an unknown amount of time which seems like forever and could turn into forever, is the worst place to be. Every moment in such a place feels like a century, and it is natural to want to come out of this place and move toward a better, brighter future for yourself. But the question remains: how do you do that?

When you are in a scarcity mindset, you sacrifice yourself, your health and wellbeing, and most of all your self-care – because when survival is in question, self-care automatically takes a back seat. When you don't pay attention to your self-care, though, over a longer period of time, that alone can cripple you and your ability to move forward in the direction of your dreams and your much deserved success.

When you don't feel well because of lack of self-care,

you not only lament yourself and talk down to yourself in your head, but it also clouds your judgment and ability to make sound decisions in your life. The decisions you make, or don't make, are the key factors that determine the quality of your life. Unclear thinking is like driving down the highway full speed with a fogged-up windshield. When it is difficult to see the road ahead, your chances of landing yourself into an accident are extremely high. This is unsafe driving, whether it is a car on the road or you in your life.

Having some income here and there from time to time can possibly sustain you in the short term. However, the costs of living, such as rent or mortgage, food, utilities, and more, are pretty regular. You have bills to pay every month. The uncertainty in income and certainty of expenses, don't go very well together. The unknown variable of income with a known variable of expenses creates a terrifying cash flow situation and can cripple any business or life situation. Staying up late at night, worrying about what to do to make it through the next month's bills is draining, and I completely understand that from personal experience.

Having sustainable income in your business and a cash flow structure that can carry you through financially, month after month, is crucial to having peace of mind in your life.

> *"Scarcity comes from living in the fear of losing. Abundance comes from living in the possibility of creating. Choose to focus on possibility and create your own experience of abundance."*
>
> — AVADHI DHRUV

CREATE YOUR TRUTH TO KNOW YOUR VALUE

You grow up hearing other people's opinions about yourself and start believing them as truth. You get conditioned into believing that what others say about you is your reality and get in the habit of looking for answers outside of yourself. When you don't find answers which seem satisfying to you, you feel like something is wrong with you. Perhaps you were just born broken, or something is missing and there is nothing you can do to change that. Thinking and feeling this way can be crippling, when in fact, none of it is true.

You question yourself and your worth: Who are you to dream such a big dream? Who are you to have a life of abundance, fulfillment, and freedom? Is this all just a pipe dream, and not possible in real life? Why do you have the gut feeling that you should go for your dreams, when you are barely getting by, and finances can't even meet to help you survive?

When you feel like you don't have the confidence it takes to be successful in business, it shows up as self-doubt and thoughts of why you can never do what you set out to accomplish. This type of negative self-talk can damage your self-esteem and should be curtailed as soon as possible.

Questions pop up such as: "Who am I to show up and create something out of nothing? How can I create something of value that nobody of authority gave a stamp of approval to?" This type of thinking can lower your self-image to merely that of a cog in the wheel who has little power beyond having to keep turning and obeying someone else's orders to survive in life. It is emotional slavery, to be completely frank.

"Self-worth is the confidence that it is okay not to be perfect and love yourself anyway."

— AVADHI DHRUV

None of the above needs to be your reality. You are in the right place, ready to learn how to change all of the above, forever, in your life. You can have unlimited growth potential for your income in your business, and freedom in your life that you always wanted, without the burnout.

After reading this book and applying the principles explained, your life will look and feel completely different. Quite simply put, you will have freedom of time and money.

You'll be able to read a book on your time or spend time in nature regularly to recharge yourself and care for your health. You'll be able to do things you love and give yourself time to do things for yourself. You may like to go hiking or go for a walk on the beach. You may enjoy a beautiful nature trail by a lake. You will not need to worry about or think twice about paying for your self-care needs. You will be able to take the time for yourself to get a manicure, pedicure, a massage, and relax to rejuvenate yourself to feel whole in your body. You will be able to give yourself permission to enjoy life's pleasures, like having a scrumptious, healthy and tasty meal at your favorite restaurant, or ordering delivery at home without worrying about how much to tip the delivery driver. You will be able to enjoy your life with peace and quiet; that is your birthright.

You'll be able to go out on dates with your partner or just with your friends and loved ones. You will not need to think about everything else that is going on, and why you can't take time off for an evening of fun. You will be able to be present with your partner and connect on a deeper emotional level because money and time are no longer constraints for you. You will be able to spend quality time with your family. You will be able to have the time and money to go on vacations, whether it is a week-long trip or even just a weekend getaway. Perhaps you may enjoy a road trip to someplace new! You will feel like you have a social life and have your tribe to connect with on a regular basis.

The ultimate dream-come-true is that you will have a business where you feel fulfilled, and where you have your clients giving you testimonials about how you have helped change their lives. You will be sleeping well at night because you are proud of your work. You will also now be able to hire help and start building a team of your own. You will feel satisfied by the kind of business you have created because of the difference it is making in your clients' lives and in the world.

Stay tuned, as the following chapters will explain more about how your dreams are indeed possible. The rest of this book is ready to walk you through, step by step, how to create your personalized plan for making your business dreams a reality in your life.

2

A TRUE STORY OF DISCOVERY – WHY YOU CAN BE WHO YOU WISH TO BE

In my early childhood, growing up as an innocent and malleable child, I was protected and cared for. Naturally, I thought that the world was a good place and that everything the people around me said and did was right. I believed that everything I saw and was told as a young girl was the correct thing to do, and that I would always be safe and protected in this way. I believed that this was the only way to live life.

Then, in my adolescent and early adulthood years, my life took unexpected turns. I discovered through rude awakenings that not everything the crowd did was right, or worth following. I realized that not everything I grew up believing was what works in the real world. I felt deceived, like I had been betrayed. I was dejected and heart-broken, as I felt lost and suddenly very alone in my quest. I started looking for what was true, or if there was such a thing as the truth after all. Since I hadn't found the truth yet, I couldn't help but conclude that the world was full of deceptions and was not such a good place after all. I started believing that the world was unfriendly and dangerous, and I had to be cautious every step of the way to keep myself safe, and not get hurt. My life got lonely in the midst of the parties and all the people around. I felt like I didn't belong anywhere, and that perhaps I should just hide from the world and not show how lonely I felt within.

At a point in my early twenties, the loneliness got too overwhelming and unbearable for me. I knew there was something more to the story of my life, because as a child I had always believed in fairy tales, magic, and mysteries. I had always been fascinated by love stories – how they always had a happy ending and a happily ever after. I wanted mine. So I went on a search, a quest for the truth. This time, I started looking for my truth in the world, and what resonated with me. I looked for what spoke to my heart. I was only interested in the songs that sang to the tune of my wishes and desires, the beauty that made my eyes dance with joy, and the wisdom that rang true to me.

THE STORY OF MY RESIGNATION

In May 2011, I graduated with a degree in Industrial and Systems Engineering from a top engineering program in the United States. Thereafter, I worked in the corporate world for three and a half years through a Leadership and Technical Development Program at Caterpillar Inc., and I gained valuable professional experience during this time.

On a sunny, San Diego day in November 2014, with unprecedented anticipation and nervous exhilaration, I confidently walked into my boss's office with a hard copy of my resignation letter. Not only was I resigning from being an engineer, I was also resigning from being an employee. I knew I wanted to go from being an employee to being an employer. The work environment at my job had started to feel like a golden cage to me. I craved freedom in my lifestyle and wanted to design my life on my terms. I felt like I had a purpose to fulfill in my life (even though I did not know exactly what the purpose was at the time). I knew that I wanted to create high-quality job opportunities for others through a business of my own from there on forward.

I gave up my car at the time to downsize by working from home. I solely relied on my savings to sustain me, and I created a budget to be able to have minimal expenses for rent, utilities, and food.

I set a goal for myself that I would build a business and create the same level of income that I had from my corporate employment, within six months after the resignation. I thought this was a reasonable goal. Wow, was I in for a big surprise. At the time, I had no idea what it would take to start and grow a business, one that would be aligned with my purpose, and which would generate enough income for me to live my dream lifestyle.

I invested my savings in several training and coaching programs, workshops, books, etcetera to learn, and ended up doing my own practical MBA from the school of hard knocks over the next two to three years. I started a private label physical products business, a digital products business, an affiliate marketing business, and learned about real estate, etcetera. I learned in depth about insurances (by working with insurance agents), tax laws and strategies (by interacting with and hiring accountants and CPAs for my businesses), legal entities and structures for business (by interacting with legal advisors, entity formation lawyers, and attorneys while forming and dissolving multiple legal entities), and I applied everything I learned. I also applied the personal wealth strategies, and the debt reduction strategies I learned.

THE SOUL-SEARCHING JOURNEY

I listened to audiobooks, podcasts, and interviews, watched YouTube videos, read every book I got my hands on, and searched for the meaning of life and my purpose in it. I was looking for the answers to who I am, why I am here, and what the goal of life is along with how to build a business, how to succeed as an entrepreneur, how to make a plan for my business that would work for me, and how to create a sustainable business, etcetera.

Since childhood, I have been a voracious reader and researcher. I've been a seeker for the ultimate truths in life. I have always believed that dreams are planted in us because they are meant to be manifested and become a reality. I knew I had a reason for being on Earth in this life, and I just needed to discover what that was so that I could align myself with it and live my life in a way that was promised to me by divine right.

I understand how it feels when you have not identified your true path and mission in life yet, because I have been there. At the time I felt completely lost and had a million questions in my mind about what I was meant to be doing with my life. I had a burning desire to find my answers and live my life in a way that was aligned with my truest purpose.

THE FEAR OF RUNNING OUT OF SAVINGS

Two to three years after resigning from my corporate job, I felt like a complete failure, and was losing my patience, because two years felt like a long time to me and I had not figured my business out yet.

After being a successful student in school and college, engineer and manager in my corporate career, and after having had a glorious professional identity for years, I was experiencing a complete loss of my professional and personal identity during this phase. Feeling like a complete failure and realizing that I had lost my identity was the most soul-crushing emotional space for me to be in. This is when I experienced "the dark night of the soul," where I felt completely lost and alone.

I was feeling the fear of running out of my savings, so I went hungry for days hesitating to order groceries or food at home. I had been depriving myself of my routine self-care needs because of the constant concern and scarcity in my mind. Living in the uncertainty, unknown, and hopelessness of where and when my next income would come from was the most difficult part of this journey.

I used to lie in my bed feeling weak, not having energy to get up and shower because I worked so hard trying to figure out how to earn an income, and yet I saw dismal results with no respite in sight.

I've been there, and I know what it's like to feel lack. I felt shame, guilt, emotional pain, disrespect, and more. My absolute nightmares were the constant questions from my grandfather (who has been my biggest role model) about what I was doing, and the nagging questions from other people, "So, what do you do?" I had no answer to those questions. So, I withdrew myself from all social interactions and lived in my own cocoon. However, I could not hide from myself, and the questions remained in my mind. I had to find the answers to them for my own peace of mind.

I've been there and have risen from the ashes as the phoenix does. In the next chapters of this book, I walk you through everything I've learned in a succinct and digestible manner, so no matter where you are in your journey, you too can rise from the ashes as I did.

At the time I was consuming all sorts of content, and one day I came across a DVD which had some interviews of self-made millionaires and billionaires by T. Harv Eker. In one of the interviews, a billionaire said that it could easily take ten years for an entrepreneur to be truly successful. Here I was, thinking that I was a failure because I had put in two long years into my entrepreneurial journey, and this billionaire was saying that ten years was not such a long time when it came to being successful in business. I was shocked. Something in me fundamentally shifted at that moment. I reframed my entire perspective to a much longer term for this journey. The billionaire in the interview said that if an entrepreneur is willing to commit at least ten years to this journey, then he or she should keep going. If not, it would be better to just quit and go get a job. Listening to the self-made millionaires and billionaires share their stories of failures, struggles, and how they overcame it all, was therapeutic for me that day. I thought that if these people could go through long periods of failures and still be successful, so could I.

Most people only share stories of their successes. You normally don't get to hear stories of people's struggles, but everyone has those moments in their lives. It's very helpful when people are vulnerable enough to share not only their successes but also their failures. Hearing the stories of people's struggles as an example of what a human being is capable of overcoming can be inspiring.

THE REALIZATION THAT I MATTER AND SO DO YOU

Through the experiences of my soul-searching journey, I realized that I matter, my life matters, and my life purpose and mission are essential to the bigger picture of the world. The unique way in which I can make a difference in the world, by being authentically true to myself, is in fact the reason why I have a soul calling. I realized that the only thing that can bring me abundance and fulfillment that I longed for is the fulfillment of my purpose in this life. These moments of light gave me the motivation to keep looking for more answers, and I continued to move toward my dreams.

I share the above because all of this also applies to you. You matter, your life matters, and your truest purpose in life is an indispensable contribution that the world needs. You have a soul calling, and fulfilling it is the way for you to achieve true success in your life. Keep this in mind as you read further.

THE QUEST FOR ANSWERS

Once, there was a man called James who was searching for something under a streetlight. Another man, David, spotted James in the middle of the night at the streetlight. David went over to James and asked him what he was searching for. James said he had lost his keys and was trying to find them.

David felt bad for James and offered to help him look for the keys. Both of them looked everywhere under the streetlight, up and down on the side of the road, but the keys were nowhere to be found.

At last, tired and exhausted, David asked James, "Where exactly did you drop the keys? Perhaps we have been looking for them in the wrong place?"

It was at that point that James said to David, "I lost them inside my house, back over there," pointing to his house on the other side of the street.

Flabbergasted, David asked James, why in the world he was looking for the keys down here under the streetlight. David wondered, if James had dropped the keys inside his house, why not look for them there.

James answered that the power had gone out in his house. Since it was very dark in his house and he could not see anything, he came outside to look for the keys under the streetlight where it was bright and he could see what he was looking at.

People tend to do the same in their lives as James did. They may have lost the keys to their inner fulfillment, their happiness and success, somewhere within their inner house. However, since it's dark in the house and they could not see anything there, they went outside and started looking for the keys under a random streetlight instead. People of course do not realize that this is what they are doing.

What are the odds of James finding his keys under the streetlight, outside of his house? How likely is it that he would find them away from where he originally dropped them? What are the odds of you finding the keys to your happiness and success outside of you? When the keys were lost within you, perhaps somewhere in the dark shadows of your inner house, does it really make sense to look for them outside of you?

THE TRUE DEFINITION OF GURU

In Sanskrit language, the syllable "gu" means darkness and ignorance, and the syllable "ru" means the one who dispels and removes it.

Hence, a guru is defined as the one who removes the darkness of ignorance from a seeker's life and illuminates their way with the light of knowledge and wisdom.

Guru is a Sanskrit term for a mentor, guide, expert, or master.

In ancient Indian cultures, a guru is more than a teacher. Traditionally, the guru is a reverential figure to the disciple or student. The guru serves as a counselor who helps mold values, shares experiential knowledge as much as literal knowledge, is an exemplar in life, and provides inspiration for the spiritual evolution of a student. A guru is also a spiritual guide who helps the seeker discover the same potentialities that the guru has already realized.

A guru-shishya tradition in ancient India goes way beyond a teacher-student relationship; it is much deeper because a shishya is more of a disciple rather than a student.

The significance of a guru in a seeker's life is paramount.

In ancient India, when a seeker was ready to learn, and grow into a greater version of themselves, the first step they would be advised to take was to look for an experienced mentor, also known as a guru, whom they could choose as their trusted guide. It is also said that when a seeker is ready to learn, their guru appears.

Per ancient Indian scriptures, the advice for a seeker is to "learn the Truth by approaching a spiritual master. Inquire with reverence and render service. Such an enlightened being can impart knowledge unto you because they have seen the Truth."

The relationship between a seeker and their chosen guru is considered divine. A seeker's relationship with their guru is based on trust, respect, and *surrenderfulness*. In order for a seeker to be optimally receptive toward the knowledge and wisdom being shared with them, they need to be open-minded and place their trust in their chosen guru. This also makes the seeker humble which is important because humility is a vital quality for a seeker to cultivate so they can have long-term success in their life. The seeker ideally must come from a place of surrender in order to be able to learn all that the guru can guide them through. In modern and perhaps more relatable terms, it can also be said that having a guru is similar to having a coach and a mentor, and the seeker needs to remain coachable in order to have breakthroughs and make progress toward their goals.

A guru helps the disciple especially when the disciple makes a mistake because at that time he or she is overcome by delusion, and therefore needs help more than at other times. The guru guides the disciple and protects him or her from making repeated mistakes. The guru's primary role is to give the disciple complete liberation – which includes freedom from karmic cycle and every other form of misery.

I was born in India and grew up among strong spiritual and cultural values in childhood. I attended a residential school in India, a *Gurukulam*, that was founded by Guruji Shri Rishi Prabhakarji. This specially designed school was operated by Guruji's trained team of teachers who provided an environment of holistic education interwoven with spiritual practices. At my school, the focus was on developing children into entrepreneurial-minded world leaders who have the humility of a saint, the knowledge of a teacher, and the wisdom of a guru. This unique upbringing has been a major propellant in my accelerated development in terms of knowledge and wisdom beyond the biological years.

During my entrepreneurial journey, I chose to hire help from coaches, and each coach I reached out to became my guru who mentored me toward my spiritual growth and financial success.

The seed of becoming a guru was planted in me during childhood by my Guruji in India. The seed grew into a sapling, and it was watered and cared for by my mentors and coaches, until it was nurtured into a fully grown tree of wisdom.

Now, having been through multiple phases of my self-discovery, self-realization, and self-actualization journey, I have dedicated myself to be a guru. I stand in service of humanity, for the upliftment of consciousness by dispelling the darkness of ignorance and creating space for the light of knowledge, wisdom, and self-worthiness. Making this choice to serve my divinely ordained role as a guru, uniquely positioned for empowering heart-centered entrepreneurs of our world, has been the most rewarding as well as the most vulnerable step for me.

I'm a guru. I'm a natural teacher and easily connect with people to lead them with compassion.

I'm ruthlessly compassionate. Because I care so deeply and am naturally empathic, I'm willing to stand for my clients' greatness, even when it means cutting through their excuses and resistance to change with ruthless compassion. I work with my clients to courageously break down their barriers and limitations in order to empower them to reconnect with their true magnificence.

IDEAL WAY TO CONSISTENTLY CHOOSE GROWTH OVER STRUGGLE

Through trials and errors, I have realized that living the life of my dreams doesn't require working long tiring hours which cause burnout. If I create healthy boundaries in my schedule and in my relationships, and seek appropriate mentorship for each stage of my journey toward the next level of growth, I can achieve any level of success I desire.

I have also realized that I can either choose struggle or growth in this journey – and the choice is always mine.

The same applies to you.

You can consistently choose growth over struggle by having an experienced guide support you in your journey. The best way to do this is to have a live guru whom you can trust. Look for someone who can not only provide resources, knowledge, and share wisdom, but also hold you accountable. A live guru can answer your questions in real time to provide insights which will help you overcome any fears you may have so you can keep your upward momentum going in your business and in life.

OVERCOMING IMPOSTER SYNDROME

Throughout this journey, I felt like an imposter. I felt like a fraud and like I needed approval from my parents, husband, coaches, or people of "authority" who were above me in some way. I was waiting for someone to tell me it was safe before I could move forward in my business. I had to learn that life isn't the same as school where you have a teacher who checks your answers and gives you a grade.

I realized that life is a journey where I am the master of my destiny and I have the incredible power to choose exactly who I want to be. I can design my life in a way that I truly want it to look like. I can take risks, engage with circumstances to learn from them, and share my wisdom with the world because that's what I'm called to do. This is exactly what living life fully looks like.

I realized that:

- I get to say how my life goes.
- I get to say who I am in the world and declare it courageously.
- I get to create and give my creations the stamp of approval so they can go out into the world and serve a worthwhile purpose of their own.

You, my dear, get to do the same for your life.

> "*Hindsight is always 20/20. This is the nature of our fluid reality, so be loving and forgiving to yourself in the present, and learn from the past to create a prosperous future.*"

— AVADHI DHRUV

BECOMING THE MASTER OF MY DESTINY

Based on my realizations, I created the brand, Avadhi.guru™, through which I help entrepreneurs realize their "why," or their true purpose for being in business. I help business owners, who feel stuck, reclaim the power in their businesses, so they can grow more prosperous, make a bigger impact, and create a life of true freedom.

As a business coach, I combine two things that may not typically go together: business and spirituality. I bring a whole-brained approach to coaching. From my engineering background, I draw the left-brained experience of organizing systems and taking practical and effective steps in a logical manner. From my creative and spiritual experiences, I draw the right-brained approach of subconscious reprogramming to create spiritual alignment and inner clarity.

As a spiritual business coach, I help entrepreneurs and business leaders reconnect with their magnificence. My clients range from brand new entrepreneurs to leaders of multi-million-dollar international businesses, and by working with me they have created beautiful transformations in their businesses and lives.

Today, my natural intuition has become an invaluable asset that I use to help other entrepreneurs succeed. All of my prior experiences allow me to speak from a place of wisdom.

I value generosity, integrity, ruthless compassion, fun and joy in my personal and professional life.

I am continuing to grow my commitment, impact, and thought leadership in the world today.

"Patience is a virtue. Infinite patience is the foundation for manifesting miracles in life."

— AVADHI DHRUV

MY BIGGEST ADVICE TO YOU

My biggest advice to you is to trust your gut on everything it whispers to you. Your intuition will never lead you astray. It will always guide you to your highest human potential and greatest destiny. Question everything that has not come to you from your intuition. There is no need to distrust, however. Always question with curiosity, and look for the deeper meaning in the source of what you have taken at face value so far. Everything in life has wisdom inherently in it. You will find it if only you look for it deeply enough.

Seek the truth, absorb the wisdom that is in every moment of life as it is happening, and don't settle until you reach the ultimate truth. Your experience of life will become extraordinarily rich, and divine through this practice.

According to ancient Indian philosophy, Moksha can be understood as enlightenment. It is simply the liberation of the soul from bondage, limitations, constraints, scarcity, anything that can hold it back from its true nature which is divine. As you identify all limitations from within yourself by questioning them, and realize your true potential by consistently trusting your gut, your inner voice over any outside noise, you will move toward self-acceptance, self-realization, and self-actualization. It is through your life's journey, and your entrepreneurial journey, that you can attain enlightenment – also called Moksha, the liberation of your soul. That is the Abundance Path through the principle of Karma Yog. Following the principle of consistent action, from a place of non-attachment to the outcome, so you can realize your true inner nature, and your divinity within. May you achieve your ultimate truth and live the abundance and fulfillment you've been promised along the way.

3

WALK THE ABUNDANCE PATH FOR UNLIMITED GROWTH

In this book, you will learn the process that I developed for more than nine years to help hundreds of entrepreneurs solve their dilemmas about how to make a sustainable income and know where they are going in their business. This book exists to help entrepreneurs create sustainable business income through a business of their dreams which is based on and connected to their hearts' desires and souls' callings (which is their Dharma in this life). If you are called to bring a vision into reality through your business, this book is for you. If you are inspired to create the dream lifestyle for yourself and your family, so you can serve the world on an even greater level, this book is for you. If you are ready to stretch the boundaries of your thinking and discover the destiny that the creator of this universe has in store for you, this book is for you. The process described in the next chapters will guide you to uncover and unleash your highest potential, so you can live the life of abundance and fulfillment you were always meant to live.

The Abundance Path laid out in this book will lead you toward your greatest destiny.

Jack had always dreamed of being a teacher and a coach in some capacity. He ached to help people when he saw them struggling with their health because of the stress they were going through in their lives. When he saw someone coaching or teaching people about living a life of health, wellbeing, peace, and joy, he found himself truly inspired. In his heart, he secretly wished, and thought, if only he could be like that person and help people in the world. If only he could inspire, influence, and motivate people to be their greatest selves, to be joyful and at peace.

But alas, he believed that he could not be that. Other people could do it, but not him. It was not possible for him to take his time away from his current work, which was his bread and butter, which his family expected him to take care of, and go following his passions. He, anyway, did not think he could make any money doing what his heart called to him to do, so that would have to just be a side activity. So, he started volunteering as a teacher in a course he liked.

This was his state of mind when Jack met me. Insufficiently aware of his heart's desires, he was too busy trying to keep up with his basic work commitments which paid his bills. Lacking the confidence to even think that a real business could be created and sustained through his soul's calling, he was not following what he was being inspired to do from within.

When my clients meet me, I empower them to see the possibility of something beyond their current imagination. When I meet them, I see through their veil of limitations and look at the essence of their being. The first time we met, I asked him to close his eyes and imagine that today was the last day of his life on this planet. He was resting in an armchair, looking back at his life and how it was lived. I asked him how he felt at that moment about never exploring his heart's desire of being a meditation teacher and a coach. How was that feeling for him? Did he care? Did it matter to him or not? It was in that instance that he realized how much this calling mattered to him. He felt incomplete without it. He felt like his life would have been incomplete without him helping people in a way that would bring wellbeing and peace in their lives.

Over the next few weeks and months, as we worked together, every time he had a breakthrough, his self-confidence and clarity went up. Jack and I worked through layers and layers of his self-limiting beliefs, thoughts, emotions, habits, patterns, and most of all his understanding of his self-worth. For example, one of the limiting beliefs holding him back was that his father would never approve of him being a coach. He felt like he would feel incomplete without his father's approval, and he was afraid to disappoint him. When we talked about the power of self-approval, the breakthrough truly freed him up to follow his heart and go for his dreams without being held back by any other limiting beliefs. Now, he has the established business of his dreams. He has created a brand, a business entity with a cash-flowing bank account from the clients he serves. He has an official business website with client testimonials, and an email system set up along with an actual team that helps him manage and grow his business affairs day-to-day. He is on his way to grow his brand presence beyond he had ever imagined possible before we had met. He creates and shares his wisdom through his original content. He is ready to be an author and publish his first book within the next year. The possibilities are endless when you flow with the current of your true self and your highest destiny. Jack is well on his way to realize his greatest potential, and when you put your mind to it, so can you.

> *"When it comes to your dreams, the only voice that matters is that of your own. Listen to your inner self, by quieting the outside noise."*
>
> — AVADHI DHRUV

REMAIN PRESENT THROUGHOUT THIS READING

Read each step of the Abundance Path ahead with your heart and mind open. Remember that your mind is like a parachute; it only works when it is open.

So, take a deep breath in, and let it out.

Take another deep breath in, allow it to open your heart, and then let it out.

Take another deep breath in, allow this one to open your mind in wonder and curiosity for what's to come in the next chapters, and then release it along with any doubts that may be in your system.

Be like an innocent child stepping into the world for the first time, ready and willing to explore. At the end of this journey, you will still have the choice to return back to your old ways of thinking, if you find that those serve you best. For the time period that you and I are together in this book, I urge you to shed those old ideas and be open to hearing something new. Be ready for something fresh, filled with love and light, that could very well change the entire trajectory of the rest of your life.

I recommend that you look for the wisdom hidden deep within each story, example, section shared in each chapter. Allow the wisdom to seep into your memories, into your being-ness, and into your essence. You will feel lighter, more peaceful, joyous, and inspired.

Let each word and the energy behind it be absorbed into your psyche just as the fragrance of a beautiful flower effortlessly permeates the entire existence of a garden.

ENGAGE WITH THE CONTENT BY DOING THE EXERCISES

I encourage you to do the exercises given in each chapter, so you can gain insights about your journey and apply the steps to your life ahead.

To start off, do this simple exercise now.

Make a list of all the things and activities that are healthy for you and truly make you happy.

For example, in my case, I love listening to soothing melodious music, spending time in nature, having fresh juices and smoothies, enjoying delicious food from my favorite restaurants of various vegetarian cuisines, spending quality time with my husband watching movies or doing creative activities like painting and crafts, helping entrepreneurs achieve peace of mind before they achieve their business success, and writing toward my books, articles and more. The list goes on.

Once you have made your list, next, find ways to incorporate at least one or two of these activities you listed, into your daily or weekly routine.

The key message in this exercise is that you need to

fill your cup completely so that it can overflow. You need to replenish yourself by adding your favorite activities to your day-to-day life, so that you can have more energy to contribute to your business and to the world.

> *"What we want isn't always what we need. We can have what we want in life, if we take care of our needs first. Recognize, accept, and put your needs before your wants, to transform your life and business."*

— AVADHI DHRUV

TAKE INSPIRED ACTION

I highly suggest that you take inspired action that aligns with your heart's desires based on what comes from your soul's calling. Don't let fears or doubts stand in the way of pursuing your passions, your true purpose, your visions, and your dreams. The dreams are planted as seeds in your heart and mind because they are meant to manifest into reality in this physical world. They are there for a reason, and that reason is your sole reason for existence. Most dreams get buried, unmanifested. Don't let that be your story. I implore you to listen to your heart, the inner voice, the silent whisper, that calls to you in the quietest hours of your day. It is the nudge or tug that you feel from within, and when you feel it, pay attention to it. Give it your all. Let it guide you, even if you don't know where the journey is taking you. Take the steps forward into the unknown, and allow the Divine Intelligence to carry you because on the other side of that journey is the promised land – your destiny, your glory, your victory, your freedom in its truest form. It is your divine expression through the brilliant uniqueness that is you.

> *"Your decisions today shape your future tomorrow, so choose wisely and choose from the heart."*
>
> — AVADHI DHRUV

ACHIEVE YOUR BUSINESS VISION WITH A STRATEGIC PLAN

Below is an overview of the steps in the Abundance Path. The process ahead is designed to take you from being in a burned-out or confused state to a state where you have clarity, confidence, and an actionable plan toward realizing your dream life as an entrepreneur.

In the following chapters, you will gain clarity on the direction you need to focus on. First, you will create your long-term vision, your key intentions and your top three goals in your business for the current year.

Next, you will unlock your confidence in showing up fully. You will discover your uniqueness through the given self-discovery exercises, and be able to make a huge commitment in your life to contribute to the world through your business.

Then you will create your path on the basis of true inner fulfillment and brand clarity by connecting with your purpose. You will create your mission statement, vision statement, and core values.

Then you will also connect with your market and your dream client. You will be able to be yourself and meet your audience where they are in an authentic way.

You will create an "I help" statement based on your vision and mission.

After that, you will reconnect with your zone of genius, which is the best way you can serve your clients. You will learn how to bring the best value in the world through your unique work and get paid in the best way for it.

Finally, you will have the tools and resources to transcend any fears that might be blocking your way. You will transcend any fears of being seen or fears of success, so you can be as grand as you are meant to in the world. You will understand the importance of chasing breakthroughs to ensure your continuous growth and expansion.

Ultimately, you will be able to honor yourself and learn the importance of being detached from any external outcomes. You will position yourself to provide the most value to the world by understanding the Karma Yog principle. You will understand how to have unlimited potential for growth in your income and freedom in lifestyle by practicing detached actions, which is the timeless principle for definitive, long-lasting success.

Before the end of the book, you will identify all the fears that can stop you from achieving your business dreams even after having your strategic plan. You will also know the main obstacles you face moving forward in this path, and your available options on how to best overcome them in order to achieve your dreams.

By the end of this book, you will understand the entire path. You will see how a life of abundance and fulfillment is possible for you, what the steps are, what the obstacles are, and how to overcome them in order to realize your dream of income, impact, and freedom. You will have clarity and confidence in your ability to have a thriving business of your own. You will have a strategic plan for your business that you like, where you have unlimited potential for growth in income, and understand your worth in your entrepreneurial journey.

It is my wish for you that you be touched, moved, and inspired by this experience. May you be beyond motivated to pursue your life purpose for the fulfillment of all that you have been born to create in the beautiful world. You have the seed of potential within already. This book will serve as the fertilizer, provide the nurturing care, and the water to enrich the soil of your mind and your heart, so that the tree of your success can grow and flourish naturally. Just as easily as you breathe in, and out, in again, and out again, you will see your life unfold in the most wondrous ways. If you are ready for this adventure, let's move forward and jump right in.

4

IDENTIFY YOUR TOP THREE BUSINESS GOALS THIS YEAR

Rose came to me with a lot of confusion that day.

She said, "I have too much to do and not enough time to do it in. How will I finish it all?"

"That is a good question for us to begin with today," I said. "Thank you for bringing this up. Let's dive into what's going on. Tell me more."

"I have phone calls to return, emails piling up in my business and personal inboxes, mail sitting on my dining table that I need to check, an electric bill to pay, and then my husband wants me to help him clean out our attic before we put our house up for sale next week. I still have no time to do the accounting for my business, and I'm just so overwhelmed, I don't know what to do."

"I see, that is quite a lot," I said. "I guess you need to do all of this, and more, all at once. Is that correct?"

"Yeah, well, not all at once. But I don't have enough time to do it, and I'm falling behind." She exhaled, still anxious, but her breath and her voice slightly slowed down at this point. Now that she had voiced her concerns, she felt just a little like her thoughts and her body had a chance to slow down compared to the frenzy she had come in with.

That was my intention as well, that from hearing her express her state of mind, she would be able to recognize and be heard, so we could respond to the situation from a more balanced state of mind.

From further conversation, we recognized that she had competing priorities, which had created an internal conflict for her, and she was feeling overwhelmed and paralyzed by it all. Which direction to focus on, and what to say "no" to was a big question mark in her mind. The decisions seemed impossible to make, and she kept spinning her wheels without knowing which direction to steer herself in. No progress, no momentum.

To sum up a well-known conversation from *Alice in Wonderland*, if you don't know where you want to go, almost any path will get you there. In Rose's case, there was precisely nowhere.

Now, she was trying to get somewhere. I could tell, she was trying hard. Yet, alas, she was getting nowhere.

Finally, I asked her the fundamental question, "Where are you going, really?"

She looked at me, puzzled.

"Where is it that you want to go?"

She took that question in and thought for a moment. She was good at taking in each question I asked her and reflecting on it before answering. "I don't know?" She answer-asked.

I must say, I was pleased to hear that response. With a light smile on my face, I replied, "That is great. Now, we can figure that out for you – together." She took a deep breath in, let it out, and finally settled down. The journey of discovery was about to begin, and I could tell that she was ready for it.

With a calm smile, I looked at her, and we uncovered her vision, key intentions, and the top three goals.

Once you know exactly where you are going, making decisions about your priorities, what to focus on and what to say no to, becomes much easier and often a breeze.

Therefore, as we begin the journey to your unlimited potential for growth in income and freedom in lifestyle without burnout, in this chapter we will focus on getting crystal clear on where you are going. You will do this by first uncovering what your long-term vision is for yourself in your business. Then you will identify what your top intentions are for this year in your business. Finally, you will clarify your top three goals in your business for this year. Having this level of clarity on what direction to focus on is the first step in the process.

CLARIFY YOUR LONG-TERM BUSINESS VISION

It is important to start with clarifying your three- to five-year vision for your business and then your top three intentions for your business this year.

According to Stephen Covey's bestselling book, one of the seven habits of highly effective people is: "Begin with the end in mind."

That is exactly the context of this chapter.

It is most important to start with the end in mind. As Stephen Covey says, make sure your ladder is leaning against the right building before you climb the rungs of the ladder.

First of all, you will need to understand deeply, through many different angles and examples, about why having clarity for the big picture and the direction of your life and your business is extremely important. You will need to understand with confidence why having clarity on your business's direction is the first step in this journey.

I'm going to tell you some stories below that will help you connect these dots.

Short-term thinking works for short term results.

Long term thinking works for long term results.

Both are important, and neither is a substitute for the other.

However, there is one major caveat. If a short-term action is damaging to your long-term strategy, then that short-term action may not be worth it.

This may seem like a puzzle; however, it is crucial for entrepreneurs to understand, especially if you are feeling frustrated in your business.

Short-term thinking is rooted in the attachment to immediate gratification. Usually, it comes from a scarcity mindset and serves well for the satisfaction of an immediate need. It works for short-term results, if that's what you are after.

Long-term thinking requires a deeper dive into what is at the heart of the entrepreneur's desire and your real why for being in business. This is a mindset which weaves the mission and purpose of the entrepreneur into the execution plan for the business growth strategy.

Long term thinking requires much deeper thought, introspection, and reflection on your true values in life. This type of thinking is challenging; hence, few people choose to engage in it.

Be warned: This is different from overthinking. Overthinking is just thinking surface level thoughts over and over with no real direction or clarity at the end.

What long-term thinking is, in fact, deep thinking that lays the foundation upon which a giant monument can be built. The longer you want the monument to last, the deeper the foundation needs to be.

Building a long-lasting business, and a personal brand, is like building a giant monument – one which is meant to last for a long time and serve the world for centuries and millennia ahead. If this is your intention in life, you must make long-term thinking your primary habit.

The world needs more long-term thinkers. Join me in this mission, to create a planet of abundance and fulfillment, to create Heaven on Earth.

STAYING FOCUSED AND GROUNDED IN YOUR ENTREPRENEURIAL JOURNEY

My husband and I were zooming down the highway in San Diego one evening in the car; he was driving, and I was in the passenger seat. We had just had a satisfying dinner at our favorite Ethiopian restaurant and were headed back home.

We noticed that a car driving in the right lane from us swerved and almost got right in front of our car. The car then swerved all the way to the other side, almost cutting over to the lane to the right of its lane. We noticed this car swerving from left to right within its lane and how it was having trouble staying in the center of its lane.

This sparked a conversation between my husband and me, where we went back to our initial stages of learning how to drive a car.

"Chirag, I remember when I started learning how to drive. Initially I had a lot of trouble keeping my car in the center of the lane," I said.

"While driving, I would feel like my car is too far on the left of the lane. So, I would turn the steering wheel to the right, trying to get to the center of the lane and stay there. However, then I would find my car toward the right side of the lane. Then I would immediately turn the steering wheel to the left, trying to get to the center of the lane again and stay there. Alas, doing that would take my car to the left side of the lane again, and I could not figure out how to stay in the center of the lane consistently," I recalled my early driving days.

At this point my husband said that when he was learning to drive, he faced a similar situation. He had trouble keeping his car in the center of the lane consistently and found himself swerving from left to right.

At the time, his driver's ed teacher told him that if he kept his eyes gazing straight ahead and looked far into the distance, instead of looking at the road immediately in front of him, it would become much easier for him to stay in the center of the lane. This way he would be able to drive with more stability.

The driver's ed teacher said that when he focused on the road just ahead of the car which was at a shorter distance, the car would tend to swerve to the sides more often.

This is applicable in business as well. When you focus on the immediate, shorter distance in front of you, it causes you to swerve left and right a lot. This is how you waste a lot of energy, and your experience overall becomes stressful. Making decisions in business becomes difficult when you only have a short-term vision for your business.

Looking far ahead into the future, with a clear direction of where you want to reach, brings clarity and gifts you the power to make important business decisions. With clarity about your long-term vision, you will know when to steer the wheel to the left, or right, and by how much. It will provide you peace of mind and stability overall. Another benefit is that, now you will have much more energy to strategize and take actions to move in the direction of your goals.

Through the above example, you can understand how and why focusing on long-term direction of your business completely changes your entire experience. This also increases the chances of you reaching your goals safely. Therefore, it is worth taking some time to define your long-term vision with clarity.

BRING EASE TO YOUR DECISION MAKING

Over the years I've attended many personal development courses and workshops. One of the organizations that I participate with is called Landmark Worldwide. Earlier this year, I was in a course with Landmark, called the Partnership Explorations course. One of the concepts discussed in the course was about being "registered" versus "enrolled." Being registered means being signed up for something and being enrolled means willingly choosing because you want to participate in something. I made a matrix and added areas of my life in each of the four quadrants – Registered and Enrolled, Registered, but Not Enrolled, Enrolled, but Not Registered, and Not Registered, Not Enrolled.

This was an interesting and insightful exercise because it showed the level of satisfaction I had in my life, based on which areas of life ended up in which quadrant.

So, I mentioned this exercise to my friend Chris. Chris takes amazing care of his car and does tons of maintenance to keep the car up as it is one of his prized possessions. I asked him, which quadrant would owning and maintaining his car fall into, and he said it would be Registered and Enrolled. He agreed that it was no wonder he always felt amazing and energized about his car, no matter what he has to get done for it, and he has a clear vision of owning his car for the long term and therefore his decisions come easily when he needs to make some. On the other hand, Chris has been telling me for years now, that he wants to quit his job of fifteen years and I asked him which of the four quadrants his job would fall into. He said it would fall into Registered but Not Enrolled. Now he saw the difference in how he felt about his car, and how he felt about the job. He did not feel confident making certain decisions regarding his job because he didn't have a clear vision of the future related to his career path ahead.

I offered Chris an opportunity to work with me for a session where we would create clarity for his goal and his overall life and career vision. He accepted the offer, and he scheduled time for the session. He said he wanted to quit his job, and I said to him, "That is what you want to quit, but what is it that you want to achieve?" He said, "Financial freedom!" And so, from that moment on we called it his goal of *Financial Freedom* and now we had a new, exciting future to move toward and further clarify.

It is important to bring clarity to your goals because if you don't know where you're going, any path will get you there, which is nowhere. So, know where you're going, and in business, nobody other than you can tell you where you should go in a way that would truly work for you. Only you can know and decide where you want to go, and who you want to become through your entrepreneurial journey.

CREATE YOUR LONG-TERM VISION

I was in a session with my client Sarah, and we started talking about her goals and clarifying them. I said, "Let's start with what is on your mind. What would you like to achieve through your business?"

She said, "I want to not be overwhelmed, overworked, and confused. I want to not feel empty within. I also don't want to feel scarcity of time and money all the time in my life. I don't want to feel low energy throughout my day."

I listened carefully to what she was saying, and to what she was not saying. I said, "I understand what you just said. What you said is everything that you don't want. My question was, tell me what you would like to achieve. What is it that you do want?"

She repeated to me, that what she wants is to not feel overwhelmed and empty within. She said that she felt like she was carrying a lot of burden from the responsibilities of her family and her work, and she felt a constant emptiness within. This emptiness within was quite overwhelming and nagging for her.

I said to Sarah, "I acknowledge you for what you are saying, but what you have said so far is everything you don't want. Knowing what you don't want is not equal to knowing what you do want."

This was key for her to understand. "Knowing that

you don't want to feel overwhelmed and empty within is not equal to knowing what you do want instead."

I continued, "So tell me now, what you do want instead?" This changed and shifted the thinking gears in her mind.

She said, "Oh, hmm...." It was evident that she had not thought of what she actually wanted up until that point. I asked her to focus her thinking in a different direction than the one she was used to.

She finally said, "What I want to feel instead is happy, energetic, joyful, full of enthusiasm all day while doing all of my work. I want to feel like I have springs in my feet, and I'm dancing, singing, throughout my day. I have childlike excitement and wonder in my life."

Now the feeling of what she wanted was completely different from the feeling of what she did not want. When she was defining what she wanted by focusing on what she did not want, the feeling was low. When she described what she wanted by saying and defining what she wanted for herself, the feeling became high and quite inspiring, motivating, and exciting.

Then we went on to document, and clarify all that she wanted for herself, in much more detail so that she could take some concrete action steps for herself in that direction. Identifying the direction you want to move toward is key, and making sure it is not disguised under the cloak of the direction you want to move away from is crucial.

I want the same for you, so ask yourself whether you are currently defining what you want in terms of moving away from something undesirable or moving toward something desirable. Moving away from something painful has a much lower energetic vibration than moving toward something exciting and wondrous. A different part of your brain and energetic mechanism gets activated when you are moving toward something desirable of your choosing. When you move away from something undesirable, you are operating from what I call, the survival mode. You are trying to survive this particular threat and just get by with minimal pain, but staying in survival mode causes suffering. There is no room for creation in this survival mode. I immediately identify when my client is operating from survival mode and bring it to their awareness so they can see it for themselves. Once they see it, they have the choice to shift out of the survival mode and into what I call, the creation mode. Creation mode is all about moving toward something of choice which is desirable. Moving toward something new, something unknown yet juicy and emotionally meaningful, activates an entirely different part of your brain called the prefrontal cortex. This is when you can imagine a better future for yourself, and live into it from your mind right away, by thought and feeling, before taking actions to manifest it into your physical reality. This is where you can get into the flow of creativity. This is the magical land of the amazing world of endless, limitless, infinite creation. As someone important has said, everything in the world is created twice – once in the human mind and then next in the physical reality.

> *"The Survival Mode is a state of being where you are in constant fear of losing your physical existence and identity. The Creation Mode is all about contributing value to others."*
>
> — AVADHI DHRUV

So, create a vision of what your life and business look like over the next three to five years from now. Create the vision with as much detail and clarity as you can, first in your mind, and capture that in the worksheet provided in the companion workbook. To access the companion workbook online with fillable worksheets, see the Gift for Readers page at the end of this book.

Create exactly what you want to have, how you want to feel, and most importantly, who you wish to become in your life within the next three to five years from now.

"The Survival Mode originates from not knowing who you truly are. The Creation Mode emanates from knowing and expressing who you truly are."

— AVADHI DHRUV

SETTING CLEAR BUSINESS INTENTIONS AND GOALS

Once you have clarity on your three- to five-year vision, it is time to create your key intentions for the current year, which would move you forward toward your three-to-five-year vision for your future.

I recommend to my clients that they clarify their top three intentions for the year first. For the purpose of this book, these could be to connect with purpose, to understand your market, and to position your business offering in your zone of genius.

Use the worksheet in this chapter to define your intentions for the current year.

Productivity experts I've learned from such as Darren Hardy say that if you have more than three big goals for your life, you have too many goals. Similarly, having more than three big goals in your business for the current year, may be too many and could dilute your attention, so I recommend to my clients that they should choose no more than three goals for the current year of their life and business.

Benefits of having clear goals defined are multiple, but the biggest one is that you get to drive with the confidence and clarity that you are moving in the right direction and can stay at the center of your lane in your path ahead. It makes decision making easy and the overall experience of your journey more peaceful, productive, meaningful, and exciting.

SMART goals provide a clear direction and action plan, so make them Specific, Measurable, Actionable, Realistic, and Time-Bound.

THE MAGIC TRIANGLE STORY

In my session with a client, he mentioned that he did not have time to take actions toward one of his three goals because he was too busy taking actions toward the other two goals. This is when I noticed that he was seeing the goals as being competitive for resources like time, money, energy, attention, etcetera.

Recognizing that it was important to shift this perspective about the goals from being competitive to being collaborative, I said to him to imagine that the three goals are each a line – and when they are separate, they are just individual lines but when you put them together, they form this triangle which I call the magic triangle of your life (or your business). When the goals come together as three sides of a triangle, each side of a triangle connects with and supports the other two sides. The whole is greater than the sum of its parts, so a magic triangle is greater and more impactful in your life than the individual three lines would have been if they had remained separate in your mind.

This perspective on how to see your three goals as ones that are contributing to each other and working toward the overall progress for your business and life, is powerful. Once again, this shifts your state of being from survival mode to creation mode – from scarcity to abundance.

Identify your top three goals in business using the goals worksheet provided in the companion workbook. To access the companion workbook online with fillable worksheets, see the Gift for Readers page at the end of this book.

DEFINE YOUR SUCCESS

You grew up taking on ideas from your parents, siblings, other role models, teachers, and people in your lives, and usually your definition of success tends to be an automatic, inherited download of other people's definition of success. This does not need to be the case for you. In fact, if you would like to create a life of true freedom and tap into your potential of generating unlimited income through your business while creating an impact for the betterment of the world, it is essential that you define your success by your measures from what comes from within you, instead of what other people's definitions are that you might have taken on. As a final check in this part of the journey, review the three-to-five-year vision you have created, the key intentions and three goals you have defined for yourself, and make sure those are completely your own, and do not come from anyone else's definition of success instead.

> *"It is not your job to make other people's dreams come true. It is your duty to create the life of your dreams and then live it fully, so that other people can have permission to do the same. This is how you serve the world. This is how you live your purpose. This is how you fulfill your destiny."*
>
> — AVADHI DHRUV

FREE YOURSELF FROM BURDENS OF THE PAST

Sarah was always afraid of setting goals for herself because setting a goal and not achieving it was crushing to her self-image and self-esteem. Not reaching her goal would be debilitating to her self-confidence and make her feel terrible about herself. She felt totally incompetent and like she was a complete failure.

She had set goals in the past, and upon not achieving them, she stopped goal-setting altogether. It was the only way she knew to avoid pain and save herself from shame and guilt she would feel otherwise. However, not having goals left her feeling directionless and lacking a sense of accomplishment that she so desperately longed for.

Come to think of it, she had never celebrated achieving the goals she did set and achieve in the past. She had never focused on the goals she did reach and had always felt less-than due to the goals she had set and did not achieve. The negative self-talk about missing her goals was too loud in her head, so it drowned every success she'd had in its noise.

When Sarah came to me, I clarified for her the real purpose of goal setting. In other words, what it is and what it is not.

"The purpose of a goal is simply to give you a clear direction to aim in," I said, with the intention of lightening the heaviness that had built up inside of her by carrying the burden of all the past unachieved goals and the guilt and shame associated with those stories. "The purpose of a goal is not for its achievement to become a measure of your success or of your true sense of worthiness in life. This is an important distinction to understand and own."

"So, I don't need to carry the load of unworthiness and failures from my past goals anymore?" She asked, incredulously, as she processed what I had said.

Taking a deep breath, and letting it out with her, I said with a smile that brought in a freeing energetic space for Sarah, "You are free to be, and experiment with life newly, and can fully let go of any past loads you had been carrying around with you. None of those past goals define you unless you continue to define yourself in those ways. What matters most is how you choose to define yourself. You may free yourself from the past and recreate your future with new wings to fly. You can define yourself as a phoenix, rising from its own ashes, completely rejuvenated and new. You may see yourself as the courageous human who can dust off the past, clean out the limiting self-talk, and freshly breathe in with a new sense of hope to dream a bigger dream."

I observed her eyes brightened as my words penetrated her being and woke up her spirit that was waiting to rise for a long time.

In that moment, she was free. She was reborn. Her dreams had room to bloom again. She was ready to set some new goals for herself, to give her a sense of clear direction in her business, and in life. She was inspired to bump up her goals to the next level. Not only that, but she also knew the true purpose of goals, and the fact that the outcome of her actions toward her goals did not determine her success and worthiness. She could now move forward with a clear sense of detachment toward the outcome of her actions. She could now focus on her goals with clarity and move in the right direction toward the achievement of the highest potential of her genius.

RAISING THE BAR FOR YOUR GOALS

"The greatest danger for most of us lies not in setting our aim too high and falling short; but in setting our aim too low, and achieving our mark."

— MICHELANGELO

"Our problem is not that we aim too high and miss, but that we aim too low and hit."

— ARISTOTLE

I always wondered what the above quotes meant to say. Now I have found my understanding of them. Here's a glimpse of the wisdom, for you to apply to your business goals.

When you set goals for yourself, there are a lot of factors that are outside of your direct control. In regard to those, things might not be predictable for you to know exactly what will happen in the future. So, it is okay to give yourself grace when it comes to the actual outcomes of those goals. The importance of setting goals is so that you can determine an action plan and the real reward is in terms of who you become in the process of striving to achieve those goals.

Oftentimes, when you set a goal and do not achieve it, you logically think that perhaps the goal was too high, and so next time you should set a lower goal in order to increase the odds of achieving it. This could turn out to be a big mistake. I would want you to set an even higher goal instead. You might think this is insane but hear this explanation and think again. The reason you did not achieve the original goal could very well be that the strategy applied to achieve that goal was itself flawed.

For example, I set a goal to write and publish a book in one year. The strategy I applied for this goal was to write the book on my own with no help from any team. When I did not achieve this goal in one year, if I had lowered the goal, it would have looked like my next goal should be to write a book in two years. That would have been a mistake. I would have continued on with the same strategy of writing a book all by myself without any help, and struggled with it for two more years, most likely still not achieving my goal. What I needed to do was to *not* lower my goal. What I needed to do was change my strategy. Now, I recommend to my clients that they bump up the goal instead of lowering it. If I bumped up my goal and set it to six months to write and publish my book as a bestseller, I would have a completely different picture and would need to change my strategy for achieving this new goal. I started looking for other options than just me trying to complete the book project on my own. I found value in having a team to support me in the achievement of the goal. I hired help, and then realized that a book project is indeed a team effort and has much more involved than what met my eye before. I got an entire team consisting of a developmental editor, managing editor, proofreader, designer, marketing experts, publisher, business coach, assistants, and an entire cheering crew to keep me going. I not only wrote and published a bestseller in less than six months, but I enjoyed the journey along the way to a much higher degree than I would have by lowering my goal and stretching it out to two years and beyond, until I would have eventually given up on it.

As another example, in the recent movie *Top Gun: Maverick*, Tom Cruise's character bumps up the goal of completing the mission for the team of pilots from being more than four minutes to a mere two minutes and thirty seconds. The seemingly impossible goal opened up the possibility of the entire team not only completing the mission in record time, but also of returning back home safely which would not have been possible with the original goal of more than four minutes. Basically, raising the bar from a timeframe of more than four minutes to just two minutes and thirty seconds for the mission created a need for a radical shift in strategy. The strategy shift is what created the ultimate mission success without losing a single member of the team, which was what the entire team was looking for.

Do not be afraid to bump up your goals, especially the ones you had set in the past and have not achieved yet.

The real reason why you have not achieved them yet is likely hidden in the fact that they require a radical shift in strategy, a different approach than the one you have been applying so far. Raising the stakes will help you explore a much better and more appropriate strategy to increase the likelihood of your success multifold. You will probably enjoy the journey much more as well in the process.

SUMMARY OF GOALS MANAGEMENT

When you set a goal and achieve it, pay attention to that success and celebrate the win. It is the recognition and celebration of those wins that will give you momentum to keep moving forward. This is how you can create positive self-talk and build confidence that propels you ahead in the tough times.

When you set a goal and do not achieve it in the timeframe you had set, first release any burden, shame, guilt, and negative self-talk around it for yourself. Always remember the true purpose of goals which is simply to give you a sense of direction. Remind yourself that your self-worth does not depend on the outcome of this one goal or any goals you have set in the past, for that matter. You can define your worth, and set yourself free from the past, so that you can create a new sense of direction for yourself with a fresh perspective and true wisdom gained from this experience.

After you dust yourself off with care, instead of lowering your standards for your new goal, see how you can raise the bar beyond what you might believe is possible for yourself at the moment. The purpose of raising the bar for your new goal is to inspire you to change your strategy and explore new ways of achieving the goal. This increases your chance of succeeding now, more than ever before.

Always remember, at the end of it all, it is the person you become through the process of reaching toward your goals that is your most important reward.

In this chapter, you have understood the importance of having a clear long-term vision and immediate goals to focus on, clarified your three-to-five-year vision, connected with your key intentions, identified your top three goals, and learned how to define your success independently from other's judgments or expectations.

5

CONNECT WITH YOUR INNER GENIUS FOR INFINITE CONFIDENCE

"I know what my goal is, but I don't feel like I have what it takes to achieve it," Rose said to me as we began our session on that warm, sunny day in May. "I know where I want to go in my business, but I don't have the confidence to do what it takes to get there."

Gauging her state of mind and where she was stuck at that moment, I responded, "It is good to hear that you have clarity on where you are, and where you want to go. Now that you have clarity on what direction you want to focus on, the next step is to get clarity on who you are from within."

She gazed at me with a hint of excitement, but still quite puzzled.

"The topic of self-confidence leads us to the exploration of your self-worth," I continued. "Having a sense of worthiness, from within, is what will create the confidence that you are seeking to be able to achieve your goals."

She looked at me with interest but did not know

where to begin this exploratory journey. She continued to stare with anticipation for where we would turn to next.

"But first, we must begin with the basics," I said, to give her curiosity a sense of direction. "Below is the foundation you will need to understand, to then be able to connect with the Source of unlimited confidence, from within yourself."

WHY MOST BUSINESSES STRUGGLE TO GROW

I was having dinner with Arjun at a Thai restaurant in San Diego, when he asked me, "Do you know why most people start a business?"

Reflecting on his context of an Indian cultural background, I said, "You mean, to make money and to put food on the table?"

He nodded in agreement, and said, "Yes. Basically, they need to survive." He was referring to the base physiological tier from Maslow's Hierarchy of Needs.

I got what he was trying to point out to me. I told him I understood.

At that moment, a thought came to me like lightning, and I asked Arjun, "Do you know why most people struggle to grow their businesses? Why do most young businesses fail to hold up?"

Puzzled, he looked up from his menu, and said, "No, I don't know."

My heart jumped with joy as the dots connected in my mind, and I said, "Hint: The answer is in the answer to the first question you just asked me."

He scratched his head for a moment, and said, "Is it because most people start a business to make money and survive?"

I nodded, yes, indeed.

"It is the survival mode and scarcity-based thinking that create struggle," I explained. "A business is not meant to be a means for mere survival. It's meant to be a vehicle for self-actualization, referring to the highest tier of Maslow's Hierarchy of Needs. A business is the means for providing greatest levels of service to the world. It is meant to bring fulfillment to the business owner, while abundance is a natural byproduct of it. In order for a business to thrive, the business owner needs to be in the creative mode instead of mere survival mode. That's what makes all the difference."

Both Arjun and I were amazed at the insight this innocent conversation had brought us. We had found an interesting concept to explore the depth of business success, over a simple meal of spring rolls, tom yum soup, and Thai curry.

SURVIVAL VERSUS CREATION MODE

You are told that it is "normal" to live in Survival Mode. That is how all the animals live. They live to eat, sleep, procreate, and die. There is no space for creation in their routines. Then why do you, as a human, have higher faculties of mind to be able to create something out of nothing? Why do you have an awareness that allows you to observe your thoughts, emotions, behaviors, and be present with your intuition? Why do you have an urge, within yourself to want to be more, do more, have more, experience more? Perhaps, you, as a human, are a higher manifestation of the Divine, and you have been gifted the talents and abilities to create and manifest the world around you in ways that only the highest power that created you can.

Why do you end up staying in and living in Survival Mode then? More importantly, why do you think that creating something as magnificent as your dreams would be possible by staying in Survival Mode?

Why don't you make a conscious effort to move from a fixed mindset to a growth mindset? From an "I know it all" to an "I want to learn something new"? From "I am a victim to life, and I must endure it" to "I am the creator of my circumstances, so let me learn how I can shape them for the benefit of all"? Perhaps, you don't understand who you truly are and what your true powers are. Or perhaps you don't realize the actual impacts of living in Survival Mode.

The Survival Mode is the state of being where you are constantly in fear and worry about your survival and existence in this physical world. When you are constantly concerned about yourself, your vision becomes narrow, and you cannot think beyond your existence and all possible threats to it.

Creation Mode is all about contributing value to others. All creativity is the expression of the Divine to bring love, joy, and celebration to humanity. Then how can creativity exist in Survival Mode? How can growth happen by staying in the self-obsessive tunnel vision?

The true impact of living in Survival Mode is that all creativity and growth is sacrificed. All love, joy, and celebration are abandoned. The pursuit of wealth and prosperity turns into a heavy burden instead of being an exciting adventure. Human relationships become a lie, inauthenticity grows at the expense of integrity and truth.

Before you know it, your whole life becomes like living a lie, and you suffer. You suffer in more ways than one – physically, mentally, emotionally, spiritually, financially, socially, and environmentally. All human suffering arises from living in Survival Mode.

The payoff, of course, is also quite compelling. By living in Survival Mode, you get to be fixed in your mindset, set in your ways, don't need to grow or change and can be "right" while making others wrong. You can be judgmental of others' actions and beliefs, while feeling like a victim all along. This resistance to change is enormous and can become harder and harder to break as time goes on.

So long as you live in Survival Mode, you are doomed to the limitations of the unconscious mind, which only reacts to the surrounding world. You are not open to any new possibilities beyond your past experiences.

In order to create abundance and prosperity in your life, you have your creative faculties to tap into, which can only open up by going beyond the Survival Mode into the Creative Zone.

When you fully get present to the impact of the Survival Mode, you can perhaps contemplate on the possibility of exploring something beyond it, of going into a Creative and Growth mode.

> *"Living life fully has nothing to do with conforming to other people's opinions and everything to do with listening to the tune of your intuition."*
>
> — AVADHI DHRUV

CONNECT WITH YOUR TRUE TALENTS

I had a client, Brian, who came to a session and said to me that he had found the *Enneagram* type list below over the internet while googling about personality traits and he went through the nine types to figure out which one he resonated with. At the time of our discussion, neither of us knew these were the nine *Enneagram* personality types that we were looking at.

He said he identified with numbers one through seven and number nine, so he has crossed off number eight type. When I looked at it all with him in the session, I recognized that he had crossed off or dismissed the one type which was his true self.

When I asked Brian why he had crossed off number eight, it turned out to be his fear which was clouding his vision from being able to see who he truly was. Ironically, it was number eight type that he had most deeply desired to be all of his life. He had the desire to be that type because in his heart of hearts, his true self already knew that he was number eight type and he had yet to recognize who he truly was, and then live up to his true potential in this life.

During the session, Brian recognized the fear which had clouded his vision up to that point. Now, looking past the fear, he saw that he is the number eight type more than anything else, and his true natural gift and potential is in the number eight type. After this realization, he felt free to be himself, his true self from within. He was liberated from the fears that were keeping him small and stuck, confined in his illusion of mediocrity.

I want the same for you. Take a look at the nine types

below, and notice which types you identify with right away, and which type you feel like "crossing off." Then examine the type you feel like crossing off, more closely. Notice if there are any fears clouding your vision regarding this type.

It is usually harder to see your fears, just like it is hard to see in your blind spot while driving. Hence, I recommend you ask for support from a trusted friend or an experienced guide for this exercise. I usually offer this type of support for my clients. Together, we uncover all the fears and doubts clouding the vision of my client, so that they can truly see what their inner strengths and natural gifts are. This way they can see who they thought they were and have been acting like versus who they truly are from within as their true self.

1. Type One (Perfectionist/Reformer): High sense of integrity, disciplined, hard-working, conscientious, purposeful, idealistic, well-organized, responsible, good attention to detail.
2. Type Two (Helper): Helpful to others, generous, supportive, warm, empathetic, caring, self-sacrificing, likable.
3. Type Three (Achiever): Goal-focused, motivating and inspiring to others, ambitious, competent, confident, adaptable; a role-model.
4. Type Four (The Individualist): Creative, sensitive, intuitive, empathetic, aesthetic sensibility, introspective, authentic to self.
5. Type Five (The Observer): Keen observer, perceptive, knowledgeable, innovative, an

expert in their field, problem-solver, curious, calm under pressure, strong powers of concentration, keeps confidences well.
6. Type Six (The Loyal Skeptic): Loyal, dutiful, committed, collaborative, team player, trustworthy, well-prepared, responsible, natural trouble-shooter, keen wit, hard-working, persistent.
7. Type Seven (The Enthusiast): Enthusiastic, optimistic, high energy, spontaneous, adventurous, engaging, connector of people, quick thinker, versatile, synthesizer of ideas.
8. Type Eight (The Challenger): Self-confident, decisive, willing to take risks, protective of others, strong-willed, charismatic, self-reliant, action-oriented, takes initiative, magnanimous, a natural leader.
9. Type Nine (The Peacemaker): Keeper of the peace, brings harmony to situations, good mediator, able to put themselves in others' shoes, affable, comforting to others, accepting.

Your natural gifts are usually hidden in plain sight and so it is often difficult for you to see them yourself. It is easy to dismiss your talents and abilities, but they can be a huge blessing to other people when you express them in an authentic way.

One of my favorite movies, as a kid and as an adult, is *The Lion King*. It is the story of how a little cub, Simba, goes through a childhood trauma of losing his father who was the King of the Jungle. After this trauma, Simba forgets his dream of growing up and being the King of the

Jungle like his father. He abandons his jungle to live an ordinary life of other animals. This story is very much like the story of a lot of humans in their adult lives.

Just like Simba had forgotten his true identity and later remembered who he was, you may have forgotten your true identity and it is now time for you to remember who you are. Just like Simba realized that he was the King of the Jungle, and that he was meant to rule and protect his Jungle community, you can realize that you are the King or Queen of your territory and are meant to lead and protect your unique community. Just like Simba recognized his duty and made a choice to live his calling, you can recognize your duty and choose to live your calling. Following the path of your calling, which is also your Dharma, will lead you toward your divinely ordained destiny.

Allow this story from *The Lion King* to inspire you toward your self-discovery. Use this example to reconnect with who you truly are, and what you are meant to be doing as part of your Dharma on this planet. When a forgotten childhood dream comes back to life, it feels just right in your heart. Similarly, when you remember your calling, it will feel just right for you. You will know without a shadow of a doubt that it is what you are meant to be doing, in this life through your business.

"Connect with the world by connecting with your true self within."

— AVADHI DHRUV

THE POWER OF PRACTICING SELF-APPROVAL AND SELF-ACKNOWLEDGMENT

As a child I was often advised that I should seek approval from an adult before attempting anything new. At the time, this was for my safety so that I would not get hurt by things I did not understand. Thus, I grew up with a habit of needing approval for everything I did, I developed a habit of seeking approval from someone outside of me, like an adult or an authority figure who somehow knew more about the real world than I did. I relied on people other than myself to tell me what to do and when.

When you grow up with this habit of needing approval from outside of yourself, from some authority figure who perhaps knows more than you, this can work in your favor when you are dealing with the outer world of complex consequences and pitfalls you need to navigate through. Asking for help and support from trusted experts and guides can be helpful in your journey to success.

However, when it comes to your inner world, discovering who you truly are and understanding your journey with clarity in this life, it becomes paramount to look for that guidance from within yourself. When it comes to your inner world, it is important to understand and practice self-approval and self-acknowledgement. Entrepreneurship can be a lonely journey, and if you are always looking outside for approval and acknowledgement, you may never find those which can leave you feeling drained. It is in those moments, when you feel depleted, discouraged, defeated, and are on the verge of giving up, that you most need to understand what is missing, and shift your perspective. I coach my clients to shift their mindset from needing approval and acknowledgment from outside authorities, to gaining that approval and acknowledgment from a reservoir of infinite intelligence within themselves. This exercise is extremely powerful for all my clients because they can now rely on a guide that is always with them, and with that support they can take action to move forward with confidence and clarity.

A client of mine, Mark, was upset that one of his customers had not given them the same amount of orders allocation this year as they had last year.

I asked Mark what he was truly upset about, and when we dug deeper, he realized that he was upset because he had collapsed the orders allocation with personal acknowledgment and was upset because he felt unacknowledged for all the work that he had put into serving this customer so far.

In the session with Mark, we uncovered and got clarity that the decision of how much orders allocation to make was a business decision and needed to be made by the customer. Mark could not control that business decision.

However, the true cause of his upset was the feeling of under-acknowledgement, which could be addressed by Mark directly from within himself. This is where we applied the concept of self-acknowledgement.

I asked Mark to close his eyes, take a few deep breaths and relax. Now, in this relaxed state of being, I asked him to imagine being acknowledged for all the work he has put into his business so far. I asked him to self-affirm, by saying "I acknowledge myself for all the work I put in to grow my business and serve my customers."

Further, I asked him to give himself a pat on the back and say, "I am proud of myself for my dedication, service and commitment to my work."

In this way, Mark recognized himself for his contribution like he had never been recognized before. Mark felt rejuvenated through this.

During that session, there was a major shift in his perception of approval and acknowledgment. He no longer needed to depend on customers, his parents, or any other people for approval and acknowledgement. He could choose to listen to his inner guidance, take a moment and acknowledge himself, and celebrate his wins from within, so he was now truly free to be himself.

He was free from the upset he originally came into the session with. This new state of being is what I call, the state of true freedom. Freedom where you are no longer dependent on things or people outside of your direct control, to define your inner state of being.

This is what I encourage every entrepreneur to embrace, so that you can take on anything life throws at you and still be grounded in your essence.

> *"Whenever you feel the need for outside approval, just choose self-approval instead."*
>
> — AVADHI DHRUV

THE ART OF EXPANDING YOUR COMFORT ZONE

You often hear that growth exists outside the comfort zone.

You also hear things like "fake it 'til you make it" but find it hard to understand and implement.

So, often when you want to create growth, you feel like you have to force yourself to step outside of your current comfort zone.

When you forcefully step outside your comfort zone, initially it may feel euphoric. Interestingly, however, an all-or-nothing phenomenon starts happening.

You feel like you have to be totally outside the comfort zone to achieve growth and success, but then when you are outside the comfort zone and something unfamiliar happens, you feel unsafe and feel like you need to completely retreat back into your comfort zone to feel safe again.

Now this all-or-nothing phenomenon starts to develop into a yo-yo pattern. No matter how euphoric it feels in the short term, it's not sustainable as a growth strategy for the long term.

This yo-yo pattern indicates that the mindset behind a particular goal hasn't been expanded yet. So, the strategic actions being taken in the short term aren't creating sustainable long-term, authentic growth.

There is a difference between the saying that growth is outside the comfort zone and the truth I've found that growth is in the process of expanding the comfort zone.

For long-lasting results and sustainable growth, it's important to not just step out of the comfort zone, but expand the comfort zone to include the new territory in the comfort and safety zone now, which earlier was outside the comfort zone.

This requires connecting with the version of yourself who is already in the expanded comfort zone and merging with that version of you to become one with it.

It requires owning that part of you who is the

expanded version of yourself, as the true and authentic version of you so you can honor it with love and respect.

Once you are one with that version of yourself who feels safe in the expanded comfort zone, you have more room to move around in. You can truly take the actions that are within the new expanded comfort zone, without having to force yourself to do anything.

Instead of being in the yo-yo pattern, now you can just be free to be you, the new expanded version of you, that is.

This is the method I recommend for creating consistent growth in an authentic and aligned way. This is what I've found to be a foundationally beautiful way of creating consistent long-lasting growth in business and life.

UNDERSTANDING AND ACKNOWLEDGING YOUR EMOTIONS

Another key to being grounded in your essence is in recognizing your emotions. As I say to my clients – emotions are energy in motion. The law of conservation of energy states that energy can neither be created nor destroyed, it can only be converted from one form to another. Therefore, ignoring emotions never leads to productive outcomes. In fact, suppressing emotions can lead to a lot of confusion and overwhelm in your entrepreneurial journey.

I also say to my clients that emotions are like important messengers that come up to show you something that you did not know was in your way. Once you can recognize, acknowledge and release what has been in your way, your journey becomes much easier. It becomes full of ease and flow after the important message from the emotions has been received.

My clients usually come in with unacknowledged emotions which are often causing them a lot of confusion, stress, and anxiety. We deep dive into it together, and uncover what emotions are under the surface of the situation they are dealing with, and after shining the light on the exact emotion that is running the show underneath the so-called upsetting situation or circumstance, my client is able to shift their perception to a new way of looking at the same situation which would be more empowering for them to move forward with.

What emotions are you harboring under your conscious awareness, which are causing you confusion, overwhelm, anxiety, or stress? Once you uncover what the emotions are, do you have some tools to safely acknowledge and release them from your body and emotional system? I have trained in several powerful tools and created my unique method called Clear Intention Healing as a tool which I use to help my clients achieve freedom from the nagging emotions and negative thought patterns holding them back. Through careful introspection, and with the help of the power of your intention, you are able to release the limiting thoughts and feelings, which turn to behaviors, and create space for empowering thoughts, uplifting feelings, which turn to empowering behaviors for your journey. If you would like to get a taste of this process, reach out to my team and we will walk you through your personalized transformation.

Using the same energy that was blocking your success, to now be a propellant for your movement toward your goals, is what I call alchemy. Since energy cannot be created or destroyed, and it takes tremendous amounts of energy to move toward your goals, you need to harvest that energy for your success from somewhere. In this case, you choose to harvest that energy, which serves as fuel to propel you forward in your path to your definition of success, from the subconscious blocks and emotions which are currently trying to keep you safe but in fact hindering your growth. It is like magic, turning copper into gold, or a pigeon into a goldfish. Together, it is possible to turn your limitations into your biggest propellants for your strengths which carry you to your success.

THE IMPORTANCE OF SELF-CONFIDENCE IN BUSINESS

In any moment of life, you have a choice between struggle and growth.

Every time you choose struggle over growth, you lose your self-confidence.

Your self-confidence is directly linked to your connection with your true self, your inner genius.

Consistently choosing struggle over growth causes you to lose your connection with your true self.

So, the way to increase your self-confidence is about reconnecting with your true self.

Every time you choose growth over struggle, you grow a stronger connection with your inner genius.

As you reconnect with your inner genius, your self-confidence automatically increases, and grows stronger.

So, in any moment, ask yourself, how can you choose growth over struggle?

Your choices create your life. Choosing your growth is

the way to creating prosperity in your business and freedom in your life.

When you are ready to make growth a consistent choice in your life, you are ready to have an experienced guide support you in your entrepreneurial journey.

To get the most out of this reading, complete the self-discovery exercises in the worksheet provided in the companion workbook. To access the companion workbook online with fillable worksheets, see the Gift for Readers page at the end of this book.

If you want to know what is truly important to a person, just take a look at their calendar and their bank account. What they spend their time and money on tells a lot about what's important to them.

So, to apply this, take an honest look at your calendar or planner or journal and your bank or credit card statements to understand what is important to you and what you're spending most of your time, money, and energy on. Take an inventory of it. It is highly revealing and will be helpful for you to understand where you have been focusing, in your life and business, so far.

The good news is that if you like the direction you are going in, you can continue to spend your time and money in the same manner. Alternatively, if you do not like the direction you are headed in, you now have the awareness and the choice to do something about it. You can choose to make some changes, allocate valuable resources like your time and your money toward initiatives that will propel you forward toward your business goals and dreams in life.

It is important that you own your success, or lack thereof, and recognize the factors contributing to it. This is so that you can make minor shifts or major redirections as to how you spend your energy, in favor of being able to confidently achieve what you say you truly desire.

THE POWER OF INQUIRY AND SELF-DISCOVERY

"Who am I?" This is the fundamental question that you need to ask yourself, yet you don't think to ask this because you have already been given an identity by others, and *you* have already bought into that as yourself.

When you buy into what society has slapped onto you as your identity, that leaves no space for you to explore that answer from within yourself. What if you were to set aside the identity you have bought into so far, and start fresh?

I recommend that you start anew with this exploration into self-discovery. Even if you have done this before, especially if you think you have already figured it out for yourself, do it newly, because self-discovery is truly an ongoing journey and not a destination. If you think you've reached it, you've forgotten that it's a never-ending process, and it's in the process that there is magic to be found.

When you get that it's a beautiful path that is always evolving, you have arrived.

So then, knowing yourself is about cultivating a habit of rediscovering the gifts and talents that are meant to be uniquely expressed through you. It is about becoming one with the beauty that is within you and all around you. Knowing yourself, your true self fully, is about creating the space for your authentic expression to show up.

"Fall in love with yourself, and you can achieve anything you wish to attain."

— AVADHI DHRUV

This exploration is the most effortless journey you'll ever be on. It is the most natural and spirited adventure you'll embark on. It is also the most rewarding outcome you'll ever achieve in life.

Are you ready to hop on this journey with me? I'm ready to be your guide, shining light in the dark places so you can see clearly, showering love on the ignored spaces so you can embrace yourself fully, showing you how to step forward into your authenticity so you can feel fulfilled and on purpose in your everyday life.

If yes, hold my hand, and let's begin.

"Confidence is not a function of knowing everything outside of you. Confidence is a function of knowing who you are within yourself."

— AVADHI DHRUV

CONNECT WITH YOUR INNER GENIUS

There are many ways to reconnect with your inner genius; use these to create even more clarity for yourself in your understanding of who you are and your direction of your life and business.

1. Be in silence and listen to the whispers of your intuition. Pay close attention to the nudges that it gives you.

2. Be present to the miracle that life is, all around you. Notice the birds singing, flowers blooming, breeze blowing as wind, trees showering their wisdom and contribution in the world. Connect with mother nature, and be present to your voice, the quiet whisper, that calls you back to your true inner nature. The joy and bliss within yourself. Be a witness to that.
3. Be in gratitude because a grateful heart is a magnet for miracles.
4. Be of service in a way that calls to you the most. Don't worry about how you will get compensated for it, just yet because that step will come just a little down the road in this step-by-step process. For right now, the priority is to get clarity for yourself on who you are and what calls to you the most. So being of service in a way that feels natural to you is a great way to reconnect with your inner genius.

Allow your life's plan to unfold in front of your eyes. ask yourself who you're truly meant to be, no matter how big or unachievable it may seem; if it is not scary, it is not big enough yet. Think big and dream bigger about your self-image.

> *"When you fall in love with your true self, you naturally fall in love with life."*
>
> — AVADHI DHRUV

In this chapter, you have learned the difference between survival and creation mode, connected with your purpose, learned the importance of self-approval, understood the nuances of your comfort zone, gained insights on self-confidence in business, and connected with your inner genius.

6

CONNECT WITH YOUR PURPOSE – YOUR DHARMA

"I had a dream that I was lost in a forest and didn't know how to find my way," Rose shared with me, as we began our session that day in June. The sun was shining bright.

"Interesting. Do you think that meant something to you at this stage in your business foundational process?" I asked.

"Perhaps it was a sign that I need to get even more clarity on where I am going along with who I am as an expression of my business, so I can connect with the dream market, my dream clients who I am meant to serve," she said.

"Great, I think that would be a great place to go deeper in during today's session." I nodded.

"Okay, so now I have clarity on my goals and the direction I am going in, and feel more confident about who I am, what my strengths are, and how I can leverage my uniqueness in my business to move toward my goals. Now the question is, how do I bring all of this out into the world in a way that my business can stand out as its own unique entity?" Rose asked, with more clarity after completing the previous two steps in this process and looking for even more clarity toward the formation of her dream business.

"Great question," I exclaimed. I was excited to see where this was going next.

"This is where you formulate a unique personality for your business. You get to create a unique identity for your business, which can also be called your brand." I continued.

The creation of your brand, when it is based on the true and authentic expression of your inner self, is an exciting, fun, and rewarding experience in and of itself.

I explained to Rose that first she will identify and understand the "why," the purpose of her business's existence. This is her business's mission, and will always give her a reason to keep moving forward in the right direction, especially when the going gets tough.

Next, she will create the vision of her business, so that she and everyone she shares it with can be clear on what her business brings to the world. The vision of her business is inspirational and motivational for her and for her team as well as partners in the future. It draws her toward it, rather than her having to push forward toward it. It also helps her identify and solve actual problems, which are opportunities for her business to truly make a difference in the world.

Finally, the core values of her brand define the character of the personality and who the business is as a true and authentic expression of itself, so that it can fulfill on the mission and accomplish the vision it has created. The core values also give her and her team a strong guideline to make business decisions and take consistent actions from.

Together, these three aspects become the mission, vision, and core values of her brand. They give her business a unique flavor, a personality which cannot be replicated anywhere else because it is her unique creation.

I finished with a smile, and she nodded with a sense of understanding and eagerness to move forward.

"Sounds interesting, but how do I create my business's mission, vision, and core values?" she asked.

Sensing her readiness, I said, "I'll walk you through it next. So, let's begin."

UNDERSTANDING YOUR BUSINESS MISSION, VISION, AND CORE VALUES

Your personal mission is your Dharma, your sacred duty and soul contract with the Divine. You may understand it as your life purpose. The seeds of this are already embedded in your being, and the talents and gifts you need to fulfill on this promise are already in your heart, which you were born with. These are your strengths and natural gifts which come easy and effortlessly to you.

Your business vision statement describes what the world looks like after your personal mission has been accomplished.

Your business mission statement explains what you do, through your business, to translate the business vision into reality.

Your brand core values are the key characteristics that you and your business show up with, so that the business you create is a true and authentic expression of who you truly are at your core as a human being. The core values together create the personality of your business.

The ancient Indian epic called Mahabharat tells the story of a warrior named Arjun, who became an Enlightened Warrior and won in the biggest war fought in the history of the Indian subcontinent.

Arjun's personal mission was to fight for justice and bring order to the Aryavart kingdom.

His business vision was a unified kingdom run by a capable team of rulers and advisors who would restore just, harmonious, and prosperity-based practices for the community of people living in the kingdoms.

His business mission statement would then be to aid and collaborate with rulers who were standing for justice and obliterate unjust rulers from the kingdom to restore peace and harmony in the communities and allow for prosperous growth of a unified nation.

His advisor, coach, and best friend, Krishna, became his guide in creating this clarity for him especially in the moment when his mind was clouded with fear and self-doubt on the Kurukshetra (land of the battle). It is this divine guidance that is called the Bhagvad Gita which explains the basic philosophy of living a meaningful and satisfying life as a human being.

According to the ancient Indian philosophy about the ultimate truths of this adventure called life, below are some crucial pillars to understand and be aware of.

Karm (कर्म) is the law of action-reaction, of taking ownership and responsibility for your life, so you can create what your heart desires.

Dharm (धर्म) is your duty, your sacred contract with Divinity. It arises from compassion and is rooted in experiencing unconditional love for all. It is all about living your soul's purpose in every moment of your life.

Arth (अर्थ) is living a life of riches and abundance. It is about sharing the jewels of wisdom arising from within you, with all the people around you.

Kam (काम) is living a life you love and loving the life you live. It is about experiencing pleasure and joy through living your wildest desires, all for the benefit of humankind.

Bhagy (भाग्य) is your destiny. It is lived by the fulfillment of your ultimate potential in this life.

Moksh (मोक्ष) is the liberation of the soul. This can be achieved through the deep understanding and harmonious execution of all of the above.

My mission is to educate and empower entrepreneurs to live up to their full potential so they can experience abundance and fulfillment in their lives. This is based on what I've realized is my life purpose, which is to create Heaven on Earth.

My brand's vision is to create a world of abundance and fulfillment by empowering heart-centered entrepreneurs to take their businesses to new heights.

My brand's mission is to help heart-centered entrepreneurs who feel stuck, reclaim the power in their businesses, so they can be more prosperous, have a bigger impact, and create a life of true freedom.

My brand's core values are Generosity, Integrity, Ruthless Compassion, Fun, and Joy.

I work with my clients one-on-one to help them create their personal and business vision and mission statements in a way that feels most authentic to them.

For example, my client Jacob's personal mission is to

spread Joy, Peace, Freedom, and Abundance to his family, community, and the world.

His business's vision statement is to create an abundance mindset in the business world by bringing mindfulness to business owners.

Jacob's business's mission is to help business owners who feel frustrated and cash-strapped, experience joy and inner peace, so they can create financial growth and build a cash rich company.

His brand's core values are Authenticity, Connection, Acknowledgement, and Empowerment.

Having your personal mission, business vision statement, business mission statement, and brand core values defined is critical to bring the level of clarity needed for you to have a strong foundation to build on top of.

Now, at this point, you may ask, why, oh why, go through this process to discover the mission, the purpose in life? Why not just live the life that society or existing paradigms have already conditioned for us? Wouldn't it just be easy to "go with the flow" of societal conditioning?

It may seem troublesome to wake up from societal conditioning and may seem "easy" to follow the crowd. However, there is an enormous price to pay for it. That price is your fulfillment.

You see, to be truly fulfilled, and authentically expressed as your true divine self, you must wake up from the societal norms and conditions, to realize your true nature from within. Rather than going with the flow of the societal currents, you can connect with your internal waves of joy and freedom which arise from your heart and soul, to experience true freedom in life.

This experience of true freedom leads to inner peace,

fulfillment, joy, and abundance in life. It creates an awareness which can be likened to that of being in Heaven on Earth in your consciousness.

In order to live full and die empty, to truly love life, and live it fully, you need to love yourself. Love and honor your true self fully, so you can live a life of abundance and fulfillment. Such a life can be created by living your life consciously, on purpose, expressing your Divinity within, and expanding its awareness all around you because you are all one.

When you discover your mission, your true purpose in life, you've broken all shackles of confinement that held you back from realizing your true nature of existence, of who you truly are.

"You can be the wizard of your dreams because the world is only awaiting you to wave your magic wand so your creation can be manifested."

— AVADHI DHRUV

YOUR DIVINE CALLING

There is a deeper message, a higher cause for this entire process. There is a reason, a divine calling, a method to this madness, that you have yet to realize.

The experience of living a life of purpose automatically, and gradually, brings in the realization that you are a divine being having a human experience, and not the other way around. You realize that you are a power beyond your physical realities, that there is more to this world than meets the eye.

You grow more curious and divinely intuitive about your nature and who you are. Now, more than ever, the question of "Who am I?" becomes relevant. Rather, it becomes a burning question, and your thirst for the answer intensifies. The need to know grows exponentially, until it occupies every part of your being, your conscious and subconscious awareness, and this process is of utmost importance.

A severe and sincere longing for self-realization is the only prerequisite to God-realization. Hence, as you reach the peak of your curiosity your awareness reveals to you in a moment – who you truly are.

It is always a blend of subtle and profound moment of revelation. You are in deep sleep yet feel wide awake. You feel alert and relaxed, in a beautiful combination of peace and quiet. You may experience bliss in this moment. You may call this experience any name you wish, or no name at all, yet this single experience becomes the unforgettable moment when you truly experienced for yourself, of who you really are.

Use the worksheet provided in the companion workbook to write out your personal and business foundation. To access the companion workbook online with fillable worksheets, see the Gift for Readers page at the end of this book.

> *"Be present to the miracle that life is, all around you. Your passion will show up automatically."*
>
> — AVADHI DHRUV

In this chapter, you have gained the tools to connect with your purpose - your Dharma in this lifetime. You have gotten deeper clarity on your business mission, vision, and core values. You have also reconnected with your divine calling.

7

BE YOURSELF TO GROW YOUR AUDIENCE

"How do I know who the right client for me is?" Rose asked, perplexed about whom her business was meant to serve.

"I mean, how do I know who to say yes to, and who is not the right fit for me?" she went on. "I know not everyone can be my client, but I feel like I can help everyone in some capacity. What I do makes a difference for everyone." She kept contemplating as she thought out loud.

"I also don't know if I am reaching the right audience now, and how to find the dream clients that I want to work with. The ones that would get what I am out to teach and guide them through. Afterall, I'm a life coach now," she said. "I just don't know if I am doing this right. You know, this marketing thing. How can I be genuine and connect with the people, the market that is for my business? If I just meet anyone and try to help them, it does not feel right. Either they are not willing to pay for my services, or they are not motivated enough to do the work. How will I ever get any stability with clients who will get the kind of results I want to help create for them?"

I could tell she was totally immersed in this dilemma.

"How will I ever make money in my business? How will it light me up, and will it help me feel fulfilled? I feel like I have a million questions swirling around in my head."

As she looked at me with anticipation for some respite, I said, "Those are some great questions, and you brought them at the perfect timing too."

"The simple way to answer all of those questions is for you to be fully self-expressed as your true, authentic self," I continued. "However, I know you want examples and details. So, we will go into all of that today."

She nodded, and her eyes perked up, as she sat up eagerly awaiting what was to come next.

THE CONCEPT OF ORIGINALITY

"Sharing original ideas is how you can build your brand and be a successful entrepreneur," I said to Rose. "That is also how you can connect with your dream audience and create a connection with your dream clients, the people you would be a great fit to work with."

"I feel like I don't have anything original to share," Rose said, in a timid voice. "I'm always afraid I might copy other people and get caught, or violate someone's rights, or worse, be seen as a fraud and basically feel like a failure. I also feel like I don't have anything creative to share, really."

I saw through her veil of self-denial and asked her a different question. "So, tell me this. Have you ever seen a mother or a father sing a lullaby to their little baby?"

She nodded, remembering her mother singing to her when she was a little baby.

"Would you, as a mom someday, sing to your baby if your baby couldn't fall asleep?" I asked. "What if none of the already created lullaby songs worked for your baby. Would you create a new one?" I looked at her, eye-to-eye, awaiting a true and authentic answer.

She took a breath in and thought for a second. Then, without batting an eyelid, she said, "Yes, of course, I would do anything for my baby! I could come up with something, a song, a line or two of lyrics, anything to lovingly help my baby fall asleep." Her motherly instincts had taken over. As women, and men, truly as humans, we have our empathic side that can show up powerfully in such moments.

"That proves that you have the ability to create and be original in your content. If you could create a song, a lullaby for your baby because you cared enough, you could create original content for your audience, your market because you care enough. It is the compassion in your being that helps you create. It is the love you have for your audience that helps you create beautiful content which exists to serve them and make their lives easier, better, happier, and richer." I rested my case and gazed into her eyes for her to realize the truth.

She had just met a side of herself that she has never known existed. Rose was shocked. Part of her still wanted to argue how business was different from being a mom, and how she still couldn't create original content or did not know how, however, now she had seen the part of her which could create if she put her heart to it. She stopped arguing against her abilities and was open to exploring the next step instead.

Gauging her readiness, I continued to explore the next set of questions that I knew still remained.

"So, that begs the question: what is original?"

I explained to Rose that if you go to the root of the word "original" it would mean something that has an origin. In that sense, everything has an origin which is the one creator that is at the origin of everything that ever existed or does exist or will ever exist.

The word "original" can also mean something that serves as an origin for something else. Everything that exists gives rise to something else, so everything is original in that sense as well.

So, what is truly original, and what is not? In my understanding everything is original. More specifically, everything that originates from within and comes straight from the Source, through you as the channel, is original. Any content that flows through you freely from Source is original. That is my definition of originality. You can take that and make it your own.

Deep in thought, listening intently, Rose nodded and said, "That does make sense. Wow, I never thought of it that way."

I saw a glimmer of excitement in her eyes.

Deriving ideas or gaining inspiration from other sources around you is natural and normal. When you can take that and add further value from your interpretations, understanding, experiences, wisdom, and then share your creation- when it comes through you, it is original from you.

Here is an important distinction to keep in mind.

What other teachers, courses, seminars, books, external sources taught you is their original content. You don't need to copy theirs. Just process it and gain wisdom from that for yourself.

The learnings, understanding, life lessons, and wisdom that you took away from applying all of that external content, the realizations you have had through your experiences, are all yours. Now you are free to share what's yours with the world.

You need to own your wisdom and share it fully with the world as your wisdom, which turns into your original content. It comes through you. Discard any confusion about what is other people's content and what is yours. Hold a clear distinction in mind and practice it in your business.

I paused to make sure Rose was still with me on this important topic.

As she nodded, I continued. I said to Rose, do not strangle your creativity in the fear of not being enough in comparison to any of the other sources. You are just as unique as they are. They need you to shine, just as much as you need their light. They've done their part, now it's your turn, and this is your chance.

In fact, in order to be a leader in your industry and in your market, you need to be a genuine and an authentic expression of yourself. In order to be the genius that you are, and express your genius out into the world as a guru would, it is essential that you share your original content with the world generously. Your full self-expression will not only influence the world in powerful ways, but will also propel your business and brand forward. Sharing your true self freely will most crucially provide you with the deep level of self-satisfaction that you have been yearning for.

The original content from you is meant to flow out

into the world through you. If you keep it hostage inside of you, it will become a bottleneck and strangle your creativity. Allowing it to flow freely will provide you the peace of mind and confidence that you need to be successful in your entrepreneurial ventures.

I could see that Rose was inspired. There was a sense of relief, and a new level of aliveness on her face at this point.

> *"All creativity is an expression of the Divine to bring love, joy, and celebration to humanity."*
>
> — AVADHI DHRUV

HOW TO CREATE BEAUTIFUL CONTENT AUTHENTICALLY?

Rose went on with her next question: "So, how exactly do I create original content that comes through me? I understand the importance of it, but how do I do it? What do I do?"

I explained to Rose that there are as many ways to create original content as there are ideas and people in the world. Like anything else, it takes practice to become skilled at creating content.

You can start with some baby steps. You can create in ways that feel the most natural to you. Some of the best ways to gain inspiration that I have found are as follows:

- Sit in nature quietly, and hear your thoughts. When you have an inspirational thought, capture it in your journal or notepad. There's your original content.

- Look at a little baby, and connect to the innocence of this being, look into the tiny eyes full of sparkle. Allow that energy to flow through you as inspiration, and capture what comes to you in those moments. It could be a thought as a quote, a picture as a vision, a lyric for a song, or just a note for a musical tune. Allow it to find you and flow through you. Be present to the beauty around you, and let it come through you as your original content.

These are some ways you can connect with your inner essence and create original content that comes from within you.

"Allow yourself to experience the freedom and joy that emerges from within yourself and flows through your heart."

— AVADHI DHRUV

Rose, with all her brilliance, came up with her next beautiful question. "What if I am not in an inspired place, and am stressed out or angry about something. Then I would not be able to create content, right? Then I would be totally stuck," she said, losing hope.

"Just note that all the questions you are coming up with are also your original content. They are coming from within you, are they not? Did you notice that you come up with the best questions when you are stressed or feeling frustrated about something? You're still creating original content." I smiled and paused for her to catch up with me.

"What? So, I can still create while I am stressed? What is the trick for that?" She asked.

I smiled and nodded. As I continued, I said to Rose that in fact, I have seen some of the best content being created when the originator was experiencing intense emotions like anger or upset. Content creation is a wonderful exercise for emotional release.

Next, I showed her how to create beautiful content authentically through the process of recycling emotions and turning that energy into her creative expression.

Let's say, something is bothering you and you are feeling angry. Anger is an intense emotion, and if you do not release it in a healthy manner, it can cause a lot of damage to yourself and others. You can channel that energy – as emotions are just energy in motion – and put it to good use toward content creation.

Take a journal or notepad and write what thoughts come to you, raw and unfiltered, just as they want to show up. Do not worry about editing anything because at this point energy just needs to flow through you, freely and uninterrupted.

If you have a specific person or audience in mind at that time, even better. Write it as a letter to them, almost like you were speaking to someone specific.

Let everything you need to say, come through you, and capture it all until you feel a complete relief in your emotional state.

When you get to a point where the anger seems to have vanished from your system, your catharsis is complete.

You will also notice that at the end, you are left with some newfound wisdom from this process of free, unadulterated self-expression. You can capture that wisdom in your original content piece as well. There you have it, your emotional energy recycled into your original piece of content.

The benefit of this method is twofold. First, you get to process through your emotions fully, in a healthy manner rather than leaving them to other destructive ways. This in itself is a huge benefit to you. Second, almost as a bonus, you get to create beautiful and authentic content which contains wisdom that you can share with the world in its rawest and truest form. That is exactly what the world, your audience, the market is looking for, from you.

You can edit the content for clarity, and put some finishing touches on it later on. Then, you can share it with the world in ways that would be beneficial for the audience.

Here's an exercise for you to do next. Use the Content Creation Exercise worksheet provided in the companion workbook. To access the companion workbook online with fillable worksheets, see the Gift for Readers page at the end of this book.

Give this method a try and share with me what comes up for you. I'd love to hear your experience of creating your authentic content, as beautiful and original as you.

> *"When you recognize your Divinity, you can tap into Divine Wisdom easily from within yourself."*
>
> — AVADHI DHRUV

BE A BIG FISH IN A SMALL POND

In 2017, I had my initial exposure to the world of coaching in the US. I had been assigned a coach as part of a personal development program I'd invested in, and I scheduled my one-on-one sessions with him every week for an entire year.

The first assignment I had from my coach was to create my mission and vision statements. Shortly after that, I talked to him about how I had realized that I was meant to write and publish my first book and become a published author.

When I inquired about how to start this new journey of living my mission and vision in the world, my coach introduced a new concept to me about marketing. He told me that the best thing to do when it comes to connecting with the market is, rather than be a small fish in a big pond, be a big fish in a small pond.

He explained that everyone usually tries to be in a big pond and ends up being a small fish in it. He said that technically, a small fish in a big pond does have access to a lot of water around, but it tends to get lost in the big pond due to the sheer size of the pond and it becomes harder for its people to find that fish in a big pond. In this analogy, the fish is the entrepreneur and the pond is the marketplace.

The truly successful people do the opposite. They look at being a big fish in a small pond. First, they find or create their small pond, which can also be referred to as their niche, and then they become the big fish, also known as the market leader, in it. They find the one thing that they can serve people in, and then develop themselves to get good at that one thing. The most successful people in the world do not try to be a jack of all trades and a master of none. They choose one trade at a time and become the master at it.

This was the first time I had been introduced to the concept of picking a niche.

A couple of years down the road, I was yet again refining my brand and business strategy.

A business coach I had hired at that time, explained this same concept to me in a slightly different way.

I was having a passionate discussion with my coach during that coaching session, when. I said, "I feel like I could help everyone in some way, so why should I not keep my marketing language generic? Why should I limit myself to a particular niche or a small group of people?

Why shouldn't I make the biggest impact I can by targeting everyone and being open to helping everyone in the world?"

I thought my question was coming from a place of wanting to be of service and make the biggest difference possible in the world. Afterall, that is my mission and purpose in life.

My coach said, "Imagine a spider web. There are many threads that are all connected together that make up the web. Now, what happens when you touch just one thread and pick it up a half an inch?"

I said, "The entire web moves up along with that one thread."

She said, "Exactly. In order to move the entire web up, you don't need to move all the threads of the web up simultaneously or one by one. The connected nature of the threads in the web is such that when you move up just one thread, the entire web will be impacted and move up automatically."

"Similarly," she continued, "when you touch the life of one particular person or one particular group of human beings, and help them with one specific area of their lives by helping them solve one specific problem they are facing, that upliftment will impact all other areas of their lives. This is because all of their areas of life are interconnected like the threads in the spiderweb. Those people you help will in turn impact other people in the world positively, and so on, the ripple effects of the work you have done will go far and beyond your direct realization. The impact of your work with the people you serve will create massive waves, and that is how your contribution can truly serve the world in a major meaningful way."

I was surprised by this revelation. I had not thought of it this way, but this made a lot of sense now that I understood it.

"Also," she went on further, "it takes deep study in one particular area for it to become your expertise, so that you can truly make a unique difference in the lives of people by solving this particular problem. When you dedicate yourself to going deep into one area and helping people solve one particular problem impacting one particular area of their lives, you can truly bring deep transformation to the people you help, in a way that the result is meaningful, impactful, and long-lasting. When you help make this kind of a difference in their lives, you make many ripples in the water by dropping just one drop of water in a still pond. Therefore, the best way to serve your purpose in life is, in fact, by focusing on the one thread of the spider web, or by dropping one drop of water in the pond which goes on to create ripples for months, years, decades, and millennia to come."

I was amazed at the newly revealed truth in this, and it made sense to me. This is how I learned why a niche is important and what its purpose in terms of marketing is.

After realizing my life purpose and mission, for the

longest time, I had a gnawing question bothering me. "I'm just one little person over here, with not much influence or power to move the huge world out there. How am I possibly supposed to make an impact that can reach the entire world of over 9 billion people?" I pondered this question for a while, and couldn't find an answer to it from the outside, which left me quite discouraged at the time. Then one day, the answer was revealed to me ever so subtly by nature, in less than a whisper.

I was sitting at the poolside and noticed that the water in the pool was completely still. I could see all the way to the bottom of the pool, and the water had no movement. Then the wind blew, and one little drop of water fell from the sky. That one drop touched the water in the pool and created a tiny ripple. The small circle that was formed from the first ripple created more ripples and grew into a bigger circle. This rippling phenomenon continued on to form bigger and bigger circles, and ultimately, the entire pool was in motion. The energy that was transmitted through one tiny drop of water into the pool of water through a single point of contact had ultimately transferred itself to the entire pool and shaken it all up.

It was there that I found my answer. In order to move the entire world of billions of people for generations to come and make a huge impact for the betterment of humanity and planet Earth, all I needed to do was be that one little drop of water that created the first ripple. That drop of water needed to have two characteristics to be able to do its part. First it needed to be its true self, its true nature of being a drop of water. Second, it needed to act with an intention of creating the first ripple. That's all. Now I asked myself: could I be the one little drop of water, true to my inner nature and act with an intention of creating the first ripple of positive impact? The answer my mind gave me was: "Yes, I could do that. That is exactly who I am – one little person, committed to being who I truly am, with an intention of making a positive difference in the lives of people I touch."

So, in that moment, I realized an important truth. My awareness shifted from that of being in scarcity, self-doubt, and low self-confidence, to that of clarity and complete self-confidence. I realized that in order to serve my purpose, all I needed to be is my true and authentic self. All I needed to have was the intention of making a positive ripple wherever I touched the lives of others. Most importantly, I realized that I was already born with everything I ever needed, and would ever need, in order to fulfill my purpose. I no longer needed to look for anything more outside of me, I was already rich within, and I was born that way.

I tell you this story because this story also applies to you.

Around that time, I read a book called *You Were Born Rich* by Bob Proctor where he explained this exact principle that you are born with everything you ever need to fulfill your purpose in life and have abundant riches, fulfillment, success that you could ever dream of.

You were already born with everything you could ever need to have the life of your dreams, and create the business and lifestyle you dream of. You already have it within you, and don't need to keep looking for your self-worth outside of you or approval from other people. You are born with unlimited potential for growth in your business, income, freedom, and lifestyle that you desire. Now let's find the perfect place where life has positioned you to create that first ripple, so that you can move the entire pool, the world, and create your unique impact for millennia to come.

Every human is a unique expression of the Divine, and you are meant to create ripples in unique ways in the pool of the world. Let's find your unique expression by connecting with your market in a way that only you could.

> "When you love yourself without conditions, the world finally gets a chance to shower love over you."
>
> — AVADHI DHRUV

A LETTER TO YOUR YOUNGER SELF

A couple of years ago, I created my autobiography book with pictures of my younger self. Each page depicted one year of my life so far, and I wrote letters to my younger self for each year as a way to give myself a birthday present for each year of my life so far. In writing this series of letters to self, I realized that there is much newfound wisdom I have now, which I could share with my younger self. I also realized that my dream clients would be people who are in a similar place right now to where I was a few years ago. Since I have been through the journey myself, I could totally understand where this person is coming from and help them see things differently now. I could share how I came through the challenges I faced at the time and got through to where I am now.

You can do the same. Your pain is your credential. Life puts you through the biggest challenges so you can be best prepared for providing enormous value to the world through your unique experiences. You can reflect on your life and then choose to write a letter to your younger self. You can also reflect further and connect with your dream clients through introspection. Use the worksheet provided in the companion workbook. To access the companion workbook online with fillable worksheets, see the Gift for Readers page at the end of this book.

CONNECTING WITH YOUR AUDIENCE

Here is an insight about entrepreneurship in general.

In very basic terms, entrepreneurship is all about creative problem solving. So, put in simple words, entrepreneurs are problem solvers.

In more mystical words, entrepreneurs are alchemists who can metaphorically turn copper into gold, or lemons into lemonade. Once again, this is all about turning problems into solutions, or something undesirable into something desirable.

Therefore, it is important for you to understand that entrepreneurship is not a fancy concept that would be hard to understand. It is simply about finding actual problems in the world, and connecting with people who are looking to have those problems solved.

Keep in mind, if you try to solve a problem that nobody wants solved, it may not work in your favor. If you don't solve any problems at all, your business is not likely to survive. If you do not have clarity about what problem you are solving and for whom, your communications are not going to land anywhere in a productive way. This is where a lot of struggles in business can come from.

So, always remember that entrepreneurship is about

making a difference for people by solving problems that they are willing to have solved.

That is entrepreneurship in a nutshell.

Next, pick one of these three areas – health, wealth, or happiness in relationship.

Test the market; do some research and see what people are willing to pay for. Also, look at what you have paid for in your life, as an example.

Who is your unique audience?

It could be based on a younger version of yourself. It could be someone you have already helped but had never thought of it as a business idea at the time.

Connect with this one person as a character in a play or a movie, and think the thoughts they are thinking, feel the feelings they are feeling when they are struggling with the problem that you will help them solve. Use the worksheet provided in the companion workbook. To access the companion workbook online with fillable worksheets, see the Gift for Readers page at the end of this book.

Stay connected to this person, your dream client, and in the next chapter you will discover how you can help this person by making the best quality of a first ripple of your impact in the pool of the world.

In this chapter, you have learned to create original content, understood the importance of being a big fish in a small pond, learned to reflect on your younger self, and connect with your dream client. Overall, you now know how to reach your desired audience.

8

GET PAID FOR YOUR UNIQUE VALUE

It was a beautiful morning when I saw Rose again.

Rose was anxious. "Okay, so how do I now take my authentic expression and get paid for it?" she asked. "I've created content which is resonating with my audience, and I love sharing it. More surprisingly, my original content helps me reconnect with my essence from time to time, when I feel disconnected from the Source within me. That is a quite amazing bonus I found in this process. Now I'm eager to learn how I can leverage my inner genius to generate value and get paid at the highest level for it."

"How much can I get paid, really?" was her question.

"I get it." I said. "You can get paid at the level of value you create for your dream clients. You can create the highest level of value for your clients by tapping into your talents, abilities, skills, and strengths which are all gifts you have been given since birth and ones you have either nurtured through your upbringing or can start developing now."

"We will cover all of that today," I said with a smile.

HARNESS YOUR BIGGEST STRENGTHS

In order for you to get paid at the highest rate possible, you need to leverage your best talents, abilities, and your highest quality of expertise in your work. Higher quality results you can create for your clients, the higher you can get compensated in terms of money for it. It is that simple. Most of us think making money is much more complicated than it is.

Money is a currency which is used for exchange of value. The more value created therefore brings in more money. If you want to have unlimited growth in your business income, you must align your business with your zone of genius, so you can create unlimited amounts of value and unprecedented levels of quality results for people you serve through your business.

Now that you have aligned with your intuition and connected with your inner genius, it becomes possible and highly probable for you to bring your genius out into the world through your truest self-expression. This chapter in the following pages will help you do exactly that.

To start off, make a list of your biggest strengths, talents, natural gifts, and genuine resources that life has brought you through in various experiences you have had so far in your journey. Use the worksheet provided in the companion workbook. To access the companion workbook online with fillable worksheets, see the Gift for Readers page at the end of this book.

HOW I WAS INTENTIONALLY POSITIONED FOR MY PURPOSE

Below is my story of how I realized that life had intentionally positioned me for my purpose. Below is how I knew that I was specifically prepared for my divine role on the world stage since way before my birth in this life. The family I was born into, the way my life unfolded thus far, every single experience I had, and every challenge I went through prepared me to be who I needed to be to serve my purpose in the world. The low self-esteem phases I went through and the confidence-breaking challenges that led me to find my way back to my true confident self have all been blessings in disguise. Every person I have met along the way in the life journey so far has been a guide, akin to an angel, who has helped me strengthen myself for my journey ahead.

When I was in a coaching program with a business coach a few years ago, one of the self-reflection exercises I did was to write out all my strengths, talents, abilities, and interests, and look back at my entire life to see what the common thread in everything that I had been a part of was.

I realized that I was born into a family that was full of business owners. My family owned a business empire that I have always been a part of. I grew up hearing about business and everything that goes with it, every day at the dinner table and during family gatherings throughout my life. Most of the other people I know, my in-laws, people in my extended community are also business owners. I was amazed at how I had not noticed this earlier. My grandfather once told me that running a business was in my blood, though I had not understood what he meant until that moment. I recognized that entrepreneurship, creating value in the world, solving problems for people, generating employment for the communities and the world through business was an integral part of my life from the beginning. I was born into the perfect place and received the perfect real-world training for it.

After being born in Mumbai, India, from fifth to tenth grade I had chosen to attend a residential school in southern part of India, which was a *Gurukulam*, a residential style school, where I was trained to be a whole-brained, all-rounded human being and a natural leader as an entrepreneur. I realized that all world leaders are entrepreneurs, as they choose to solve particular problems they spot in the world, and they lead a movement for creating transformational and sustainable change in the world through their thoughts, ideas, and solutions created through their thought leadership. I went to a school which was designed by Guruji Shri Rishi Prabhakarji, specifically and intentionally for creating powerful world leaders, and the environment and curriculum of the school was special and uniquely crafted according to the ancient Indian tradition of the guru-shishya *parampara*. I realized that Guruji Shri Rishi Prabhakar had blessed me as a young child, to grow up and become a world leader and spread my message through entrepreneurship all over the world.

This was how all the dots connected into a thread for me, which showed why I was so drawn to entrepreneurship, and why I was attracted to creating a business of my own which would create true freedom for me.

At the beginning when I resigned from my corporate career, I had thought that entrepreneurship would give me freedom of lifestyle where I could choose my own schedule and the type of work I did. While it is true that being an entrepreneur gives you the flexibility to set your own schedule, be your own boss, take vacations when you want, set your prices and give yourself a raise when you want to, there is a reward that goes way beyond these seemingly lucrative benefits.

I have realized that it is the true freedom which is the ultimate reward of being an entrepreneur.

The true freedom that I now realize I craved is the freedom of my own, inner, most authentic self-expression into the world. In the seven-chakra system, the fifth chakra at the throat is called *Vishuddhi* chakra that stands for finding and having a voice. I felt that I had opened this chakra on the day when I recorded my first guided meditation. I felt liberated because I had found my voice. It is a priceless reward that you get when you open up your voice and feel the freedom to fully express yourself, exactly how you are and feel no restraints to what you can or cannot say, and how you can or cannot express yourself.

So, what is the common thread for you in your life? Look back at your life and allow the hidden treasure to reveal itself to you, so you can also find your true freedom of self-expression and connect to that as your zone of genius through your business.

BECOME PRESENT TO YOUR GIFTS

Become present to your gifts, talents, and your zone of genius, keeping in mind your purpose and market identified now.

When I was doing a lot of soul searching, and I asked myself what was the most natural for me when it came to helping people, what was the most satisfying and fulfilling for me – the answer that came to me was healing. Now, I have never thought of myself as a healer, and I have not gone to school to learn any healing techniques. Yet, I felt like I could naturally create a powerful healing presence where healing could occur, with the power of my intention and thought alone.

When you realize your natural gifts, you may or may not have gone to school for or gotten any training or certification for them, but they will feel truly normal and natural to you.

They will feel real, and you will feel completely confident from within, in leveraging them to create true and lasting value for the people you wish to serve the most through your business. Connect with and recognize those talents and abilities of yours, which you were born with, and feel the most natural to you.

"Your income will only grow to the extent that you choose to show up in the world truly as you."

— AVADHI DHRUV

DEVELOP YOUR PERSONAL BRAND IN THE WORLD

Based on what your unique intuitive guidance tells you, create your unique expression in the world and name it what you wish to name your brand.

Develop your personal brand in the world; what is unique about you that would serve the world? What has life trained you to be, from all your life experiences? What is your unique expertise?

"Genius, you are you! When you choose to be yourself, your true self fully, you can be a guru for the betterment of the world."

— AVADHI DHRUV

Utilizing your entrepreneurial style, what is your unique zone of genius that you can offer the world through your business?

What do you believe? What are your values and beliefs that you can tap into, for service to your clients?

Finally, complete this exercise. Define and how exactly you can best help your dream client with the problem they have which you are uniquely meant to help them solve. Create an "I help" statement that specifically describes what you do, in one simple sentence, so that from here on forward you can use this as your introduction. You can use your "I help" statement to answer the question people often ask in social situations. When someone you meet asks you, "So, what do you do?"

You can say, "I help [insert who your dream client is] who [insert a specific problem], achieve [insert the specific inner world result you help them achieve] so they can have [insert what the dream client outer world desires after the specific problem has been solved]. This "I help" statement is similar to your business mission statement; in fact, this version would become a more specific version of the business mission statement now.

THE IMPORTANCE OF EQUAL ENERGY EXCHANGE IN MONETARY TERMS

When I started coaching, I helped people for free and it felt good to start off with because I loved coaching and helping people. However, I could not figure out why, despite my best efforts, this type of help was not creating long-term results at the level that I knew was possible. Eventually I realized that rather than helping, what I was doing was trying to rescue people, and that was energetically draining to me and was not truly helping the people I so loved in the best ways possible. When I was depleted energetically, it was difficult for me to give value to others. I needed to have ways to fill and refill my cup first.

I also did not think of the people I was trying to help as my clients. I did not think of the services I offered as a part of my business. My professional identity, my business's professional entity, my relationship with clients through clear agreements, and the concept of setting healthy boundaries for my time and energy were all completely non-existent. Living this way was heavily taxing to my body and mind, and it caused me to burn out.

I realized the importance of an energy exchange instead of it being a one-way street where I was constantly giving. Then, I went from giving away my services for free, to exchanging services almost like a barter system. This felt better than before because then I received something in return and I did not feel completely depleted like I had felt previously. However, soon enough I realized the trap in this arrangement which is that the energy exchange was not exactly equal. An energy exchange is important, but it only works when it is an equal energy exchange. For example, if my services are worth $250 and I'm exchanging them for brand strategy or design services which might be worth $100, that exchange is not balanced. Even if my services are worth less than the worth of the services I'm being offered, I will not be able to receive the full value of them and recognize the value and the exchange will not last long. Instead of this barter style exchange, what I recommend is that you set clear boundaries with a written legal agreement which includes the pricing and other terms and ask the other person to do the same.

Another lesson learned was that when you engage in a barter-like exchange, where services are being rendered but no actual money is being exchanged, there is a receiving block at play for actual money. Seeing the money come into your bank account has a much different feeling than just exchanging services. If you ever exchange services, instead of skipping the monetary exchange, set your price for your service that you offer and receive that in your bank account, while you can also agree to a price for the service that is being offered to you and pay for that in monetary terms from your bank account as a separate transaction. The ultimate cash inflow and outflow may even out if the prices are the same for both services, but the feeling you will have and the boundaries you will set around each service will be completely different. It will also make you a better accountant for your financial and cash flow decisions in your business.

REALIZING THE DIFFERENCE BETWEEN VOLUNTEERING AND A BUSINESS TRANSACTION

Joey came to me as a client who was providing services on a volunteering basis, basically free of charge, and was not thinking of it as a potential business idea or transaction.

I asked him why he was doing this volunteering activity, and he said it was because he enjoyed helping people in that way. I sensed that there was a part of him that did enjoy it, but there was also a part that wanted to run away from responsibility.

I asked him, how would he feel if he offered a free session, and people signed up for it, but then there was a no-show on the day of the session. When nobody showed up on the day that he had set aside his time for it, and spent his energy in preparation for the session, how would that leave him feeling. He answered honestly and said, "Not good. I would not feel good about that."

"What would you do in that case?" I probed further. "Do you think they have much skin in the game if they have not put their money and made a commitment to it?"

He said, "No, they would just show up when it was convenient for them, and not show up when it wasn't."

"So, is that okay with you?" I asked. He realized that he was not okay with that. He wanted to help people who would show up with commitment, and so he needed to start looking at volunteering a little differently.

"Here is another angle to look from. If you were providing a service on a voluntary basis, and you did not feel like showing up one day, would you reschedule or cancel the session that day?" He nodded, yes, he would just not show up because he is doing a favor by volunteering and nobody can force him to show up when he does not feel like it.

"Alternatively, if someone had paid for your services, and then you did not feel like showing up that day, would you be likely to back out of it?" I asked. "No, I would make sure I showed up, or communicate my emergency well in advance in a way that works for my client. I would be much more responsible and answerable to show up for my client." He responded.

"Exactly my point. When there is a monetary exchange, both the recipient and provider of the services are more committed and show up with a higher degree of responsibility toward their energy exchange in a way that works. When the monetary exchange is missing, the level of commitment tends to go down, especially when the work in the session involves emotional discomfort such as coaching does. Volunteering has its place in the world and works well in certain functions. However, you are the best judge for whether volunteering your services is the best way for you to help people and the best way for people to receive your help." I completed my spiel with that. At this point, Joey had woken up and thought in different ways about his real ambitions and how he wanted to contribute his energy into the world. He thought about structuring his services as a business, a heart-centered business, which was a vehicle for him to bring the best value from within himself into the world.

This is how he went from just volunteering his time and energy, to thinking of his services having value to be part of a real business, and taking actions to create actual business income through his services.

> *"More time does not equal more value. Higher quality results equal more value. Always be result-oriented and seek to provide greater value. That is the way to creating abundance and fulfillment."*

— AVADHI DHRUV

HOW TO PRICE YOUR PRODUCTS AND SERVICES RIGHT

Ron came to me with his coaching services package structure, and his only question was, "How much should I price this at?"

I said, "That is a valid question, and the answer lies within you so let's explore. How much do you feel would be reasonable?"

He said, "I don't know." His judgment was clouded at that moment.

I explained to Ron that the pricing for his products and services depended on two factors. First is his level of confidence in the value he creates and the worthiness he feels from within himself. Second is the level of need there is in the market for a particular problem to be solved which he offers a solution to.

I said to him that he can address the first factor by feeling into himself, how confident he currently feels about the value he brings through his services.

I also said that he can address the second factor by offering what he feels is the right price based on the first factor, and test how the market reacts. He can also look at what the market is currently paying for this type of problem to be solved. He might get a full range from this research, but then he can set the price to what is acceptable to him first and then his client as well next.

Ron was able to choose a price that felt right to him at that point, and his first clients accepted it. He was in business.

A couple of months down the road, Ron had served his initial clients and felt a lot more confident about the value he was bringing through his coaching services. He decided it was time for him to raise his pricing levels, and so we addressed his first factor – his confidence level in the value he brings through his services, and then raised his prices. He signed his next client at the higher price point just as easily as he had his original clients at a lower price point.

He had learned that as long as he feels confident in his level of pricing based on the value he provides, and the market agrees to meet him there, the price is always right.

> *"Work hard on self-improvement. Work smart everywhere else."*
>
> — AVADHI DHRUV

In this chapter, you have learned to harness your biggest strengths, understood the importance of positioning yourself in your zone of genius, become present to your gifts, and gained wisdom on developing your brand to serve your clients in the best ways and receive compensation at the highest levels possible.

9

SHINE YOUR LIGHT

"I feel like I am the world's best kept secret," Rose said. "Why aren't my dream clients coming to me?"

"Do they know you exist for them?" I asked her.

"Probably not," she said, admittedly. "How will they ever know?"

"When you show up in front of them and let them know, then they will know," I said. Quite obvious, yet it was hard to see from the other side where Rose was.

"Oh my. That feels scary to me," she said, frightened by the thought of showing up in front of people.

Fears of judgment, of being misunderstood, of not being good enough, all welled up inside of her.

"I completely understand," I said, with a kind smile, energetically embracing Rose in a compassionate hug, gradually soothing her aura to be in a safe space again.

I explained to Rose that I remember, before I ever had my business and personal brand, I had always thought that I was going to be in the background, quite like an invisible hand who would be supporting people and helping out from behind the scenes. I would never come out in the forefront because I didn't want to shine too bright. I had thought that it was somehow noble for me to not step out into the limelight, so as to not disrespect others. Later I realized that all this was my fear trying to keep me safe by keeping me small. I also realized that I was meant to shine bright and that was the best way for me to be an example, so that others around me could feel free to shine bright as well. My strategy since then has completely changed. Instead of being small so that others would not feel small around me, I choose to shine as bright as I possibly can, so that others can also be inspired to shine brightly and show up fully in their genius.

I shared my story with Rose, as she listened intently.

"Now, what has your strategy been so far, and what will it be going forward?" I asked her, putting the ball back in her court.

She smiled, heaving a sigh of relief, and asked a wonderful question: "It has been to stay safe and small, and going forward, it will be to shine as brightly as I can. How exactly do I do that?"

I said, "We will go over all of that today."

So, we explored fears that hold you back, and how to transcend them so you can show up fully to connect with people, and attract your dream clients directly to you.

HOW TO MEASURE SUCCESS

"As an adult, how do you usually measure your level of personal success?" I asked my clients in one of the group sessions.

"Usually by comparing ourselves to other people we see around us," said the group.

"Got it," I said. "Now, let's explore this a bit further."

"Imagine a tomato plant. A fully grown tomato plant usually has a height of about three to four feet. Whereas an oak tree has the capacity to grow in height up to seventy feet. Now, if you see a tomato plant that is at a height of three to four feet, and an oak that has grown to a height of five feet, when the oak compares itself to the tomato plant's height, the oak will feel that its personal success is greater than that of the tomato plant. At that point, the oak stops growing further, and calls it a day. Now, tell me," I said to the group, "which one has achieved a higher level of personal success in this case – the fully grown four-feet-high tomato plant or the five-feet-high oak?"

The group immediately said, "The tomato plant."

I said, a bit puzzled, "However, the oak is five feet higher in comparison to the tomato plant. Why do you answer the tomato plant?"

The group started thinking and said, "Because the tomato plant has grown to its full potential. The oak has not grown to its full potential of seventy feet yet, and it is still just at five feet."

This was a major inflection point in the conversation of this session.

"Exactly," I said. "And similarly to this example, measuring your success by comparing to other people's success is like comparing the height of a tomato plant and an oak tree. That would be inaccurate. Instead, the accurate way to measure your success is by measuring it against your full potential and no one else's."

So, the key question now comes up. "In order to measure your personal success, you need to know what your full potential is first." I said, "Yes, and then the question becomes – do you know what your full potential is?"

Oftentimes, you have forgotten what your true potential is, and hence, you don't have any scale to measure your level of personal success with. You have lost your way, and you keep comparing your success with other people's success instead. True fulfillment can only come from achieving your true potential, and it can also be found in the relentless pursuit of it. Success and true freedom can also be achieved by achieving high levels of personal success. The first step here is to go within, access your superconscious mind, your higher self, your heart and intuition, which always knows what your full potential is, and understand who you are meant to be. A tomato plant or an oak tree.

Once you understand your full potential, be it and you'll be free.

THE FEAR OF BEING SEEN

The fear of being "seen" runs rampant in society today, but if you think about it, just like most other fears, it is totally absurd.

It's like saying, "I'm afraid of having an arm."

There is nothing inherently scary about having an arm. Same with being seen.

It's natural, it's normal. You have a body, so you have an arm; you exist so you are seen.

It's obvious, and yet, we spend enormous amounts of energy trying to deny this reality.

You must know that no matter how hard you try the invisibility act, you'll never succeed. You must realize that it never works.

All the drama of being invisible, being behind a veil, is all an elusive untruth.

The truth is that you exist only to be seen and heard, truly and fully.

The truth is that people see you, wholly and truly.

Whether you see yourself or not, whether you are willing to step up or not, people see through your veil, they can see it in your eyes, in your language, in your being-ness, every single day.

The magic, then, is not in somehow stepping out to be seen. It's in getting that the invisibility act of yours isn't working. It can't work, so stop wasting your time and energy on that.

See yourself first. Look at yourself, connect with your true self.

Look in the mirror and gaze into your eyes, you'll always find a glimpse of your magnificence there.

Once you connect with your deeper self, gently and firmly, commit to being who you are out in the world. Know that you're not hiding from anyone, rather only deluding yourself by acting like you don't matter. Stop it and step into your light.

Take back your personal power and be the light that you were born to be in the world.

Take baby steps, but never again pretend to be someone you are not.

You are not meant to play small, so don't.

You are meant to be seen, so show up like you're the brightest star in the universe.

Show up, and shine, shine, shine!

> *"You are not meant to play small, so don't. You are meant to be seen, so show up like you are the brightest star in the universe."*

— AVADHI DHRUV

REPROGRAM YOUR MIND TO MANIFEST YOUR BUSINESS REALITY

The conscious mind is volitional and lives in the past or future at all times, rarely rests in the present. It can use discretion to choose which way to go or not go. It has about 1 to 5 percent power to direct the course of your life. It can process information at forty bits per second.

The subconscious mind is the powerhouse that drives 95 to 99 percent of your life on a day-to-day basis. It is a storehouse of memories, information, thoughts, feelings, behavior patterns, and data from many generations ahead and beyond your life. It does not choose which way to go, rather it executes on whatever has been programmed into it so far, and it can process information at the speed of 40 million bits per second.

Survival mechanisms that reside in the subconscious mind usually want to keep you safe in your comfort zone, but growth requires expansion beyond your comfort zone. So understanding the role of the conscious mind and subconscious mind programs, as well as doing the work to bring the subconscious mind in alignment with your conscious mind when it comes to your long term vision, current year intentions, and top goals is crucial to your success.

The various ways of subconscious programming are as follows.

- Learning through absorption during early years (zero to seven) of childhood
- Learning through repetition of affirmations and actions until they become habits
- Meditation with a goal or Self-Hypnosis – best results come through practice
- Psych-K® is a powerful tool to create conscious and subconscious alignment with the permission of your superconscious mind. This is the tool I use with my clients when it is called for.
- Leveraging the power of your intention through Clear Intention Healing. This is a method that I've created to help my clients.

"Your words and actions create your circumstances and reality. You are at the cause of your reality, not at the effect of it."

— AVADHI DHRUV

Your belief systems are the source of where your thoughts emerge from.

Your thoughts and feelings create your "state of being."

Your "state of being" impacts your words (language) and actions.

Your words (language) and actions ultimately create your circumstances, and your reality.

Believe it or not, you are at the cause of your reality, not at the effect of it.

The manifestation process is that your inner world creates your outer world, and your actions are the bridge.

Inner world consists of your beliefs and perceptions, thoughts, and feelings; outer world consists of the SMART goals you want to achieve. The actions you take are the bridge between the two. Your strategic plan can give you the path to walk on, and the actions to take for your business success. Now it's up to you to take the actions and achieve the results.

> *"Your beliefs shape your reality."*
>
> — AVADHI DHRUV

I have included some Affirmations and powerful Belief Statements in Appendices A and B at the end of this book, for your reference. I highly encourage you to use those, or create your own empowering belief statements, to plant seeds of abundance, prosperity, success, and peace in your life.

> *"Your beliefs can easily lead you toward your goals, if you choose to consciously align them to empower yourself."*
>
> — AVADHI DHRUV

ORGANIZING YOUR BUSINESS PRIORITIES

As you climb your way to higher levels of success, each rung onward and upward will require you to get more and more organized within yourself and outside in your surroundings.

Each step forward will call to you to work smarter, not harder. It will ask of you to produce higher quality results to the problems you help solve in the world. This will also create a prerequisite that you set clear boundaries for yourself and stay true to who you truly are.

The more intimately you get to know yourself, your true inner essence, the better equipped you will be in not only achieving success, but also in maintaining it and ongoingly reaching higher levels of it in your journey. The key to continuous growth in your success is your personal growth and understanding of yourself and how you work best, and then honoring your true self.

Say to yourself often, "Even though I have not [insert what you have not done or achieved that you wanted to], I choose to completely love and accept myself." Repeat this statement to yourself several times. Give yourself a big self-hug while saying this single statement to yourself as naturally as it flows out. Self-acceptance is also about self-forgiveness, and forgiveness comes from understanding.

For example, I was supposed to wake up at 8:00 a.m. this morning and start writing this chapter for my book. I did not wake up at 8:00 a.m., and I stayed asleep till 2:00 p.m.

Part of me totally would beat myself up and call it a failure and lack of discipline and that I couldn't do it. However, I understand that my chronotype is Late Bear and that morning hours provide me better sleep, so what I was doing was not just sleeping but deeply resting. I was getting the much needed rest for my body and mind so that I could show up fully and write this chapter with ease and grace. This was necessary for me to create the highest level of value for my reader, you.

So I applied the above technique for myself this morning. When my mind beat myself up, I said to myself, "Even though I did not wake up at 8:00 a.m. today per my writing schedule, I completely love and accept myself." In my mind, I gave myself a big self-hug, and continued, "Even though I feel like I am behind on my writing schedule today, and even though it seems difficult that I would be able to make up for the seemingly lost time, I still powerfully choose to completely love and accept myself, exactly as I am and who I am." When I said this, the thoughts of who I truly am bubbled up in my mind.

I had thought of myself as a failure before this exercise, but now I realized that who I am is a person so committed to creating value in the world that I have taken the time out of my weekend to write this book and share wisdom with the world. I am proud of myself for being this highly committed person. I give myself the time and space to rest and recharge completely, how ever that needs to look because I deserve it.

So, what is something that you have not yet acknowledged yourself for? Who are you truly, and what are you committed to, more than anything in your life? Release any thoughts that might be beating yourself up over petty things you have seemingly not done right, by first declaring to yourself that you completely love and accept yourself. Then, allow who you truly are and what you are committed to, to bubble up to the surface of your mind. See yourself as the magnificence that you are. Believe in your greatness, your true commitments to yourself, your life, and the world, more than any mishaps from the past you cannot go back and change. Your choices today determine who you are and the results you will create for yourself tomorrow. Don't ever be confined by the past choices and keep yourself small because of those petty things you can't control anymore. Understand yourself, accept yourself fully, and move forward with a new sense of confidence in who you truly are today – defined by only your commitments for your future, and nothing else.

> *"Every time you have a breakthrough, notice that it comes from a place of higher self-worth."*
>
> — AVADHI DHRUV

Finally, being open and willing to receive the abundance that you desire, is the biggest challenge and the greatest opportunity you can leverage in order to live the life you truly wish to live.

STORY OF THE DROWNING MAN

There was once a man who lived in a small town, where a huge storm hit and caused a flood. Water levels were rising, and the man's house was completely submerged in water. He somehow got to the top of his roof and stood there, hoping and praying for God to save his life.

He had been devoted to God for his entire life and was not about to forsake his faith in this testing time in his life.

One of the people from his town came by his house in a boat and called to him, asking him to come down from the roof and get into the boat.

The man refused, saying, "I have faith in God. God alone will save me."

After some time, the waters were rising further, and another boat came by for his rescue.

The man refused again, saying, "I will stay until God comes for my rescue."

Finally, another little canoe comes by, offering him a chance to get away from the house before the rising waters take over the town completely.

"Come on, this is your last chance. Rescue yourself," said the canoe operator.

"I will only be saved by God," said the man, and remained on his roof, until the water swept him away, and eventually, he drowned.

As the story goes, when the man directly met God after his life had ended, he asked God, "Even though I held my faith in you, why did you not save me?"

God said to the man, "It was me who came for you three times, with two boats and a canoe. I came for your rescue, though it was you who chose not to rescue yourself. I was always there for you, even though you may have not recognized me."

There is also a beautiful story of the footprints in the sand, which is one of my favorites.

The person asks God why in the most trying times of his life, there was only one set of footprints in the sand. God said, "It was then that I carried you."

Whether you have faith in a higher power, or not, it is paramount that you choose to have faith in yourself. Divinity is within you, and you have the power to choose to rescue yourself, or not. You have the power to believe in yourself and make choices to propel you forward toward your success, or not. The power of will, the power of choice, is always with you. Your destiny is waiting for you to unlock it. All you need to do is step into your power, and choose yourself, truly and fully, above all. Be open to receiving the abundance that is already all around you, but you may not have recognized it yet. When you see it, claim it and it's yours. You need to recognize who you are as a divine being having a human experience, so you can claim the abundance and freedom that is your birthright.

> *"Miracles are possible and can be real for you only if you choose to believe in them."*
>
> — AVADHI DHRUV

Constant change requires course correction in strategy, identifying the priorities by finding out what is the biggest constraint and the weakest link in the chain based on Theory of Constraints, to continuously strengthen your business in an upward trajectory.

The Theory of Constraints and Psych-K® tools help people overcome their biggest limitations in the context of individual goals, and when people transform their limiting beliefs into empowering beliefs, they can transform themselves to the next level.

With repetition over time, this process identifies and improves upon the weakest links (parts of oneself), which as a result makes the entire chain (person) stronger.

PERSPECTIVES ON PRODUCTIVITY

Masculine productivity is about efficiency.

Efficiency is about getting a task accomplished by consuming the least number of resources (time, money, energy, etcetera). It requires focused attention. You're pretty much well trained in this by traditional world systems and corporate structures. Progress in this manner probably looks like a straight arrow hitting the goal within the smallest number of resources every time.

Feminine productivity is about effectiveness.

Effectiveness is about making sure you are focusing on the right things at the right time and prioritizing the right projects from a bigger picture perspective. It is about listening to intuitive guidance, being aligned with overall vision by being in the flow. This requires being in sync with cycles, and progress looks like an upward spiral instead of a straight arrow. From productivity perspective, there is no point in doing something efficiently that doesn't need to be done in the first place. Hence, knowing what to focus on creates effectiveness, and this is where feminine productivity plays its part. Then focusing on it and getting it done with the least number of resources creates efficiency, and this is where masculine productivity plays its part.

Both are important; hence, my vision is to create and practice a holistic approach to productivity out in the world through the products and services my brand offers.

Depending on your entrepreneurial style, you may be most naturally inclined toward one or the other, and you probably need to rely on other team members for creating balance with the other type of productivity. If you are purpose driven, feminine productivity may come more naturally to you, and if you are ambitious and visionary, masculine productivity may come naturally to you.

The entrepreneurial styles and masculine or feminine productivity explanations are just guidelines to help you understand how you are best suited to channel your energy. At the end of the day, you are the expert in your business, and you know yourself the best, so use these tools as guides, and apply them to help you in the most effective ways as they suit you and your business.

An important lesson I have learned about productivity is to have the discernment to be able to procrastinate with a clear intention. This strategy can also be called purposeful delay. Learn to ask yourself whether something must be done today or can it wait till a later point in time. If it can wait, set it aside and focus on what truly needs to be done today. Purposeful delay of a task, in the interest of another more urgent and important task to be focused on now, is not laziness or procrastination in the bad sense of the term. It is a great productivity strategy. Utilize this to your advantage and you will not be left with burnout in your entrepreneurial journey.

> *"Progress and procrastination can both be deceiving when based in fear. Progress may come from cutting corners, and procrastination can feel like stuck-ness when based in fear. Progress feels like freedom, and procrastination feels like purposeful strategy when based in self-confidence."*
>
> — AVADHI DHRUV

BECOME UNSTOPPABLE IN THE FACE OF YOUR CIRCUMSTANCES

My clients often ask me how they can have continuous growth and improvement become a natural part of their lives and business growth. I have found a way to incorporate this which I call Chasing Breakthroughs.

Whenever you find yourself in a place of decision about what should be your next step, and have lots of ideas, ask yourself, which one idea, if you pursued it, would bring the biggest breakthrough for you. What one thing, if you did it, would expand your comfort zone, and create personal growth for yourself. Identify that one thing and do that one.

Continuously choosing the one thing that brings you the biggest breakthrough, over time, has a cumulative effect. It creates momentum of growth, and growth creates ongoing success. This is the key to maintaining and consistently increasing your level of personal success and success in your business. Chasing breakthroughs creates an upward spiral of abundance, growth, and peace of mind for you in your business. This is the best gift you can give yourself in your entrepreneurial journey ahead.

There is only so much that can be explained in a book. When I work with my clients, I help them create a truly personalized business growth strategy by applying all of the concepts mentioned in the chapters of this book.

"Consistent growth is simply about chasing breakthroughs. Breakthroughs happen when you step outside your comfort zone."

— AVADHI DHRUV

In this chapter, you have understood how to measure your success, learned about the fear of being seen, and know the importance of your conscious and subconscious mind for manifesting your business reality. You are also aware of how to best organize your business priorities and have learned to become unstoppable for your ongoing success.

10

HONOR YOUR VALUE

"How do I stay motivated each day in my business?" Rose asked, as we began our session, "I feel like every time something does not go my way, I feel discouraged and a part of me wants to give up."

"Excellent topic for today," I said. "Staying motivated, taking inspired actions consistently, and not giving up in the face of adversity are key to entrepreneurial success."

"Today, you will go deep into what truly causes disappointment and discouragement in business and in life. You will also learn how to, once and for all, overcome that trap." I said to Rose.

"Wasted time is an illusion, don't buy into it. It's either a productive use or a learning experience, and both come to fruition eventually."

— AVADHI DHRUV

The way I explain this is through the traditional ancient Indian principle of Karma Yog. Karma means action. Yog means the union (of mind and spirit). Karma Yog is a principle with which you can take consistent actions, in a way that creates a sustained union of the human mind and the infinite spirit, which fuels ongoing actions leading to success.

> *"There is no such thing as failure. Be proud of all your 'failures,' because it is the wisdom from those experiences that will uplift you toward your biggest success."*
>
> — AVADHI DHRUV

KARMA YOG PRINCIPLE

Karma in Sanskrit means action.

Kama in Sanskrit means desire or attachment.

Nishkama in Sanskrit means without desire or attachment, hence, in short it means detachment.

In a session with one of my clients, Emily, I asked her, "If you were attached to a particular outcome, of gaining an order from a customer, and if he did end up sending that order to you, how would you feel?" She said, "I could feel elated and happy."

"Yes," I said, "and what kind of actions would you take from that feeling?"

She said, "I would call more customers, do some more work and be excited to do more sales calls and growth activities for my business."

Then I asked, "And if he did not end up sending that order to you, how would you feel then?" Emily's energy dropped immediately, and with a mellow tone of voice, she said, "I would not feel good about that. I would feel dejected, and disappointed."

"Got it," I said. "And now, what kind of actions would you take from this feeling?"

She said, "I would not feel like doing any more sales calls or any other growth activities for my business. I would probably just shut everything off and leave."

This is the trap many of us fall into. "So, do you see how, allowing the outcome of someone else's actions to determine how you feel within yourself can determine your actions or lack of actions, which can determine the direction of your business success or failure?"

"Yeah. But how can I control this situation?" She asked, puzzled.

"You're right, you can't control the situation." I said, "Though you can control how you feel as a result of the situation."

"How so?" Emily asked, intrigued.

"Tell me, if you had no attachment to gaining the order from that customer, if you were in acceptance of whether it was sent your way, or not, then how would you feel when you received it?"

She scratched her head for a moment because this was a new way of thinking for her. Emily thought for a moment and said, "I would not feel elated or sad, but I would probably be grateful."

"Nicely done," I said. "And if you had no attachment to gaining the order from that customer, then how would you feel when it was not sent your way?"

She said, "If I had no attachment to it, then I wouldn't feel sad or upset. I would accept it as is and feel at peace with the opportunity to serve more customers out there. I would be able to send love and blessings to that customer and be open to receiving orders in the future when there may be a need and move on to serve other people. I would totally be at peace."

"Wow, what a difference," I said, "And how would your actions be different in both these scenarios?"

Emily said, "My actions would remain the same either way. I would feel at peace and would continue to do my work of making more sales calls and doing further growth activities for my business. The biggest difference would be that I would have peace of mind for myself in the scenario when I was coming from detachment to the outcome."

This is a classic example of *Nishkama* karma.

Life and business are full of moments of decision and taking actions.

You may take an action, or not take an action – either way, the laws of karma – action-reaction, apply. The way to transcend the action-reaction loop, is by releasing the attachment to a particular outcome, and just taking actions or not, from a place of peace and non-attachment. This is the key to unlimited potential in income growth and freedom in lifestyle for yourself and in your business, for the rest of your life.

I work closely with my one-on-one clients to incorporate peace and non-attachment in their day-to-day life, which automatically propels their business success in immeasurable ways. When you implement the principle of *Nishkama* karma in your life, you are practicing Karma Yog, as Shri Krishna explains in the *Bhagvad Gita*, to his devout friend Arjun.

> *"By giving up attachment to the outcome and the timing of it, we can allow the seemingly impossible to become reality."*
>
> — AVADHI DHRUV

HOW TO CREATE ABUNDANCE AND FULFILLMENT

> *"A heart-centered entrepreneur believes that business is about people and the planet. For this person, business is a vehicle to create abundance for humanity and to care for the planet we live on."*
>
> — AVADHI DHRUV

Here's a story of two types of entrepreneurs: a brain-centered entrepreneur and a heart-centered entrepreneur.

The differentiation begins with the basic beliefs that each type of entrepreneur holds in their mind.

A brain-centered entrepreneur believes that business is about revenue and profit. For this person, business is a vehicle to create wealth for themselves, and they hope that the wealth will also bring happiness to them in the end. This person yearns for wealth because they are yearning for happiness and satisfaction, but they believe that happiness comes from having more and more wealth. This person uses their brain to achieve what they want in life.

A heart-centered entrepreneur believes that business is about people and the planet. For this person, business is a vehicle to create abundance for humanity and to care for the planet. They know that they consistently experience fulfillment in their heart and soul from creating this type of positive impact in the world. This person is rooted in compassion and unconditional love for all. This person strives to become the best version of themselves and achieve their highest potential in life.

Both types of entrepreneurs are ambitious and want to grow their businesses.

The foundational difference in their beliefs of what business is about, creates a completely different set of questions in the minds of each of these types of entrepreneurs.

The ever-pervading questions in the mind of a brain-centered entrepreneur are, "How can I grow my business's revenue through sales?" "How do I increase my business' profits?" "How can I grow the equity in my assets and turn them into passive income or turn around to sell them for more money?"

The ever-pervading questions in the mind of a heart-centered entrepreneur are: "How can I create more jobs for people?" "How do I improve the quality of employment I have created so far?" "How do I create new products and services and improve the current offerings to positively impact planet Earth?"

The focus on revenue and profit numbers is important for keeping the financial health of a business in good order. However, when this focus on numbers becomes an emotional obsession, the business can become an addiction and a self-destructive machine for the entrepreneur and for the entire world.

When the focus is shifted to people and the planet, all the important financial numbers and metrics automatically get taken care of, and they are used for their true purpose, which is to be an aid in strategic planning and important decision making in business.

Therefore, here are the three steps to living the ultimate life, a life of abundance and fulfillment.

Step One: Give your entire life to the upliftment of humanity and the positive transformation of the world. Surrender your existence for the biggest cause of creating abundance and fulfillment for humanity and the world. Commit to being a heart-centered entrepreneur now and in the future for the rest of your life. Love the world.

Step Two: Live every day, as a heart-centered entrepreneur, and align your thoughts, words, and actions with the intention created in Step One. Conduct your business according to the foundational beliefs of a heart-centered entrepreneur, make decisions from the place of creating abundance and fulfillment in the world. Live your love for the world.

Step Three: Celebrate in your day-to-day life, enjoy each moment and live life king-size, with pleasure, love, and joy. Gift yourself all of the best that life has to offer. Allow others to enhance your health, wealth, and happiness because you are the greatest asset in your business, and you need to take care of yourself so that you can ongoingly contribute to the world in the biggest ways possible. Love yourself so you can love the world even more.

> *"A heart-centered business is a natural creation of a conscious, connected, divine entrepreneur. Be it and be free."*
>
> — AVADHI DHRUV

LOVE AND HONOR YOUR PURPOSE

There are many misconceptions about the word "love." For the purposes of this book, I will refer to love as the greatest power above all. Love is the life force that connects everyone. It is unconditional and divine. You live in a sea of it.

You may or may not feel connected to it at any given moment, but that is where "honor" comes into the picture.

Honoring love is about allowing the infinite life force to flow freely. It is about quieting the outside noise and being with your true self. Honoring love is about being present with your intuition, and connecting to that part of you which loves you beyond measure. It is about honoring yourself like a child does when he or she is playing in a pool, splashing water around freely with no concern and with total abandon.

You know how to honor yourself as children do because you have been a child at one time.

Love and honor go hand-in-hand together because love is the power that connects and heals, while honor allows that power to flow freely and fulfill its purpose. When you trust yourself, your inner nature, to be pure and peaceful enough to connect, miracles happen.

Magic appears to be real because it is the way your intuition speaks with you.

As an entrepreneur, you have the power to reshape humanity and this planet's future. You can do it in a way where you spread love and peace by tapping into your true nature, by loving and honoring yourself.

What is the purpose of your life?

This question may often come up in various opportune or inopportune moments of your existence. Sometimes this shows up as a fleeting thought, while other times this single question can become the all-pervading focus of your life.

Why are you here, in this life and on this planet? What are you meant to be doing? Who are you supposed to be being? What is the real reason for you being alive?

If and when these questions emerge into your daily awareness, you are ready for the answer to reveal itself to you.

This is when the answer to "why love your true self?" becomes relevant.

There are many benefits to loving your true self. The primary benefit applied to the whole of your life. In fact, it is only by loving your true self that you can connect with your true purpose in life.

When you love yourself, the divine wisdom within you becomes one with the superconscious power that is meant to flow through you for the fulfillment of your purpose in this life.

Hence, when you love yourself, your true self fully, you fall in love with life. You live fully, you stand tall, you feel 'on purpose'. You contribute toward the manifestation of the Divine that is seeking its expression through you. You become the vehicle, the channel for divine creation, and that is what is your purpose, your mission, your calling in life.

When you choose to love and honor your true self fully, you become an undeniable, powerful force of the divine expression. You become the light.

If you haven't already looked at Appendices A and B, I have included some Affirmations and powerful Belief Statements for your reference. I highly encourage you to choose at least five statements from that list (unless you have created your own, in which case you can use those), and start using them today. This is a way you can fuel your mind with positive and self-loving thoughts.

Repeat your chosen belief statements every day for at least one week and observe the changes you feel by doing this exercise.

OWN YOUR WORTH

My client Henry came in feeling anxious one day.

"I'm not sure how I will deliver value to my first client, I don't have enough experience or value to give," he said.

"Do you have a faucet in your home?" I asked.

Puzzled by this question, he thought for a second and replied, "Why, yes, I do."

"So, when you want to wash your hands and need water, you turn on the faucet, and water flows out, correct?" I went on and asked. Henry nodded yes.

"Where does that water come from?" I asked him further to go deeper in this inquiry.

He thought for a moment and said "It comes from the water tank in the house. The reservoir of water."

"Oh, so the water does not come from the faucet itself?" I asked, probing him to think over this again.

Henry said, "The water comes through the faucet, but not from the faucet. The water comes from the tank, the reservoir which has plenty of water."

"Great, so let's understand the distinction between the role of the faucet and the role of the reservoir in this case. The faucet is just the channel through which water is transported, but the faucet or the pipe is not what water comes from. It comes from the reservoir. If the reservoir was to be completely empty, the water would not flow through the pipe, and the faucet. Even if the reservoir was full of water, but if the faucet or pipe was disconnected from the reservoir by any chance, the water would not come through when you open the faucet. Now, if you find that water is not coming through the faucet, what would you need to do?"

"Find out where the blockage is or reconnect the pipe to the reservoir so the water can flow through the faucet again," he said.

"Exactly," I said. "So, when it comes to serving your client in the session, are you playing the role of the faucet or the reservoir? Which one are you?"

Henry was stumped by this question but stayed with me. "I ... am not sure. I was thinking that I need to be the reservoir and was feeling anxious because I feel like there is no water (value) in me. I feel empty."

"So, let's look closely, and see whether you need to be in the role of the faucet or the reservoir. Let's say the reservoir is the biggest wealth of knowledge, wisdom, value that there ever could be. Would that be you? Who would that be?"

"That sounds like it would be the divine power that created us all. It would not be me, little human by myself," he said. "So, in that case, I'm the faucet?"

"Yes," I said, "you are in the role of a faucet, a channel that, when connected with the divine reservoir, can bring unlimited value to the world. However, you need to remember that when you start feeling empty, it's not because you are the one bringing the water. Just like a faucet does not bring the water itself, it just connects itself to the reservoir and transports water through it, you are capable of connecting to the divine unlimited source of knowledge, wisdom, love, and peace, and then you can easily allow that wisdom and value to flow through you. The way each faucet is unique in its expression of how it brings the water out, you have your unique expression of value you can provide to the world, to your clients through your business. You must remember that you are just the channel, and when you connect with the Source of all value, you can never be empty again."

"So, when you are with your client, the only thing to focus on is to be the channel. Be connected to Source and know that you don't need to bring the water, also known as value. The water, also known as value, will automatically flow through you when you are connected to the Source, and coming from your true essence."

Always remember, you are unique in the way only you can express the divine wisdom through you. The wisdom from within yourself is the greatest gift you can give to the world.

Be the channel and deliver abundant value to the world. When you serve the world abundantly, the abundance will naturally flow back to you.

Following the moment of self-realization, there is an automatic phenomenon of connecting with higher consciousness, the spirit within becomes one with and becomes part of the Divine whole. In this moment, you know you are a divine being as part of the whole. You are connected to all of it, and it's all within you, as your true self glowing in its vibrancy, brilliance, and enormous magnificence.

In this moment, it also becomes clear to you, that you are worthy of Divine grace, and all that is divinely bestowed upon you is abundant. Perhaps for the first time in this life, you become present to the beauty, and the infinite source that you are connected to in all its magnificence.

You truly claim your essence, your freedom, your birthright, your well-being, and your abundant wealth and richness of mind. You own your inner peace and true nature of bliss, and allow it into your life.

Your self-worth is self-evident and automatic as you reckon the power of who you truly are and what you are a part of. You find yourself naturally in awe, wonder, and devotional gratitude, as you find yourself surrendering to all that is.

You no longer feel the need to remain in control of your life, as you pass over the control to the divine whole, with the deep realization that the sailboat of your life is in divine blessing, and the sails of that boat are best navigated by the winds of the divine blessing, while you continue on the journey of divine service, to humanity and the world.

Your life is no longer yours alone. After this point of surrender, it belongs to the entire world and the divine existence.

> *"You are the greatest asset in your business. Love yourself so you can love the world even more."*
>
> — AVADHI DHRUV

THE ULTIMATE GIFT IN LIFE

To come to this point takes enormous courage, and sacrifice from your false self. Your false self is the self-identification often referred to as the ego self. Against all odds, you have made it here, on the other side of the veil.

You are now on the other side of the illusion of separation. Now, you see the world as whole. You see yourself as whole and complete. You see divine perfection all around. When you experience connectedness with and Divinity in every living being on the planet, you are officially a self-realized being. You become a conscious, awakened human. This is what it is like to be the enlightened one – the Buddha, as you walk upon planet Earth with an open heart, in service to humanity.

You seek to bless every being that comes your way. Your heart melts at every possible interaction with another being of light, whether they are awake to this reality yet, or not. You wish to sing with the birds, dance with the trees, fly with the butterflies, and spread love and joy to all.

You find yourself in the beautiful balance of giving and receiving. As you progress through your life ahead, it feels completely fresh and new.

This is the ultimate gift in life. The ultimate gift of your transformation into pure love. When you bless your soul, you bless the entire existence. You bless the world so it can raise you to new levels of awareness every single day and unleash the greatness within you for the greater good of all.

When you choose to love yourself, you give permission to other people to do the same for themselves. This way you inspire them to also live their ultimate life.

In this chapter, you have understood the principle and concept of Karma Yog, learned how to create abundance and fulfillment, connected to the importance of love and honor, gained the confidence to own your worth, and learned about the ultimate gift.

11

READY TO CREATE SUSTAINABLE BUSINESS INCOME?

The scariest word in business can quite simply be "competition." You have probably heard phrases like, "The competition is fierce in that industry," or, "You have to stand out of competition to stay in business." You might have also heard of things like, "You have to define your Unique Service Proposition – your USP – and communicate that to the market." You may have wondered, what is your USP? When you don't know what makes you unique, and when there is already a sea of people doing the same thing that you want to do, how in the world do you do something unique? How do you stand out of the "competition"? It can seem like a hopeless endeavor, an uphill battle where there is almost no chance of survival.

So, you may think, why bother? Why go after your dreams and create a business? If business is a zero-sum game where in order for one to win another must lose, then it becomes a scarcity-minded game. It leaves no room for fun in it and becomes a constant struggle of "who has the most market share." In that type of world, the only way to gain market share is by taking away another person's share. So, you either have to keep fighting against "competitors" for market share, or just give up when you don't see a way out.

I'm here to tell you that there is a way out, and there is a world where business does not have to be a struggle and a constant survival game in the face of "competition." Dare I say, I can prove why business is not a zero-sum game (audacious claim, I know), and that it can be fun and exciting where you get to create new solutions and make the world a better place in your unique way. Business can be done with compassion and care for people and the planet. This is what heart-centered entrepreneurship is about.

> *"Your biggest 'competitive advantage' is your own essence you were born with. It's hidden in plain sight. When you understand this, you can do wonders through your business."*
>
> — AVADHI DHRUV

LOGIC VERSUS EMOTION

In my sessions with clients, I take on fear like it's nobody's business.

Often, my clients come into a session, thinking they're acting from logic, and I help them unveil the fear underlying their logic, which is what I call "logic-covered-emotion."

There's only one thing more dangerous than being emotional while making business decisions.

It's thinking that you're coming from logic, when you're coming from "logic-covered-emotion."

Logic-covered-emotion looks like logic on the surface, but as you dig deeper into it, it turns out to be an emotion. Usually, it's an emotion like fear, which causes a disempowered state of being for the client.

So, first I identify the truth of the matter, the state of being they are in. Then once the truth is clear to them, they create a transformation to shift the dis-empowered and fearful state into a confident and empowered state of being.

This is transformation because the shift is fundamental, foundational, and permanent.

Next, I encourage my clients to make key business decisions from their new empowered state of being, so they can take deliberate action steps for their business growth.

That's how you create abundance and fulfillment in the lives of entrepreneurs, and eventually for the world.

> *"Every time you have self-doubt, be reminded that your higher self has the big picture, and is fully in control of your destiny, so then you can just relax."*
>
> — AVADHI DHRUV

THE FEARS OF FAILURE AND SUCCESS

As they say, fear can easily stand for False Evidence Appearing Real.

When there is fear of failure and fear of looking bad underneath the surface of your conscious mind, it can often show up as real-looking evidence of why you should stop from taking a particular action which would otherwise move your business and life forward toward your dreams.

This fear of failure can cripple your growth because of the lack of right actions which are needed to move forward.

It can often show up as imposter syndrome, or feeling like a fraud. The fear of "what if I fail" can keep you stuck, in the name of safety and security, which is perceived to be within your current comfort zone. The moment you think of stepping outside your comfort zone, the fear, which is driven by your survival mechanism, crops up and rears its head. It makes all kinds of justifications about why you should just stay where you are and not take that action.

Now, when this happens, often I find that my clients try to either ignore or subdue that fear. They try to overstep or sidestep the fear, and push through anyway. However, in the long term this does not work in their favor. Whenever I notice this is happening, I dig deeper into this during sessions.

The client and I first go deeper into what the fear is, why it is there, and what message it has – exactly what it is trying to say. I empower and encourage my client to look at the fear and just hear what it has to say, from an objective perspective. Once I have created the space for the fear to exist, and come through with its message, when the client looks at it objectively, it becomes clear that the fear's justifications and rationale aren't true. As it becomes clearer that the evidence that fear was showing up as is not in fact the true probability, then the client is able to allow the fear to be released and let go from their system.

It is only when you give enough space for the fear to speak its part, and hear it out objectively, that you can then allow it to be fully released and diffused from your energetic system. Now, the fear will no longer be present under the surface of the client's conscious awareness. It would be released and transformed into a new state of being called peace and confidence for the client. This newfound wisdom, understanding, and confidence the client has gained allows him to think objectively about the real impact of his action and the probability of achieving the success he desires as a result of that.

As if the foggy windshield just got completely cleared, my client is now able to see the road in front of him clearly, and decide whether to turn right, left, or keep going straight.

Decision making in business becomes much easier, when you can see your path ahead clearly. Fear of failure can often cloud your judgment by fogging up the windshield of your car, so it is important to recognize when this is happening, uncover and allow enough space for the fear to completely be acknowledged, released, and transformed into a powerful empowering new state of being.

> *"Making choices from the heart may not be logical but will always lead you toward fulfillment of who you truly are."*
>
> — AVADHI DHRUV

"Our deepest fear is not that we are inadequate. Our deepest fear is that we are powerful beyond measure. It is our light, not our darkness that most frightens us. We ask ourselves, 'Who am I to be brilliant, gorgeous, talented, fabulous?' Who are you not to be? You are a child of God. You're playing small does not serve the world. There is nothing enlightened about shrinking so that other people won't feel insecure around you. We are all meant to shine, as children do. We were born to make manifest the glory of God that is within us. It's not just in some of us; it's in everyone. And as we let our light shine, we unconsciously give other people permission to do the same. As we are liberated from our fear, our presence automatically liberates others."

— MARIANNE WILLIAMSON, *A RETURN TO LOVE: REFLECTIONS ON THE PRINCIPLES OF "A COURSE IN MIRACLES"*

This quote has deeply impacted me, and I hope these words and the deep meaning behind them will serve to inspire you as much as it has me.

MONEY BLOCKS (FINANCIAL THERMOSTAT)

You have a financial comfort zone, which you can understand in terms of a financial thermostat. The way a thermostat works is that whenever the temperature of a room goes above or below a particular threshold which has been set, the hot or cool air kicks in and tries to bring back the temperature within the set range.

Something similar happens when your financial

status goes above or below your set comfort level. Unless you intentionally choose to expand your comfort zone, the automatic survival mechanisms from your subconscious mind, which are designed to keep you "safe," kick in. The survival mechanisms drive you into taking actions that would keep you in your financial comfort zone.

When you are looking to grow your income through your business, your financial thermostat setting can either become your best friend or your worst deterrent. Usually, when you are aiming for higher financial success than what you have seen in your immediate circles, like your family or close friends, you might find that your financial comfort zone keeps you stuck and will not allow you to grow your income beyond a certain point no matter how hard you work for it.

I have expanded my financial comfort zone and continue to do so regularly. I help my clients do the same, every day. It is important for you to recognize what your current financial comfort zone is. Then you will need to consciously choose to expand your comfort zone to the level of income that you desire. Through this process, you will find that attracting and retaining the amount of money you desire will become much easier for you. It will become more natural for you to retain the money that flows to you than you ever imagined possible.

GROW YOUR INCOME AND EXPENSES FOR BUSINESS SUCCESS

Generally, entrepreneurs think that if they want to create growth in their business, they need to focus on increasing income.

While this may be true and makes logical sense, there

is an interesting thing about expenses that you may be missing out on.

If you truly want to create consistent, long-term, sustainable growth in your business, it is extremely important that you focus on your expenses.

Depending on which category the expense falls into, you may need to either eliminate, minimize, maintain, or even increase expenses for the business growth.

This thought process, of increasing expenses (the right kind), for creating sustainable business growth, can seem counterintuitive, and emotionally challenging.

Yet, this is key to create an upward spiral of wonderful growth in your entrepreneurial journey.

Four types of expenses in business:

- Destructive expenses: These are expenses that are damaging your business and these expenses should be eliminated as soon as possible from your business. Example: Extra fees, customer complaints, etcetera.
- Protective expenses: These are expenses that are necessary and provide peace of mind for you in your business. These expenses should be in place and be minimized based on your business's needs. Example: insurance, legal entity, legal agreements, etcetera.
- Maintenance expenses: These are the basic operational expenses. These expenses should be maintained on a healthy balance for business to operate smoothly. Example: salary/wages, office space, utilities, etcetera.
- Productive expenses: These are required for growth of the long-term business. These

> expenses must be proactively increased
> because they are an investment into the
> business which brings in an ROI for the
> company's long-term future. Example:
> personal growth, marketing, sales, brand
> strategy, continuous improvement of systems
> and processes, networking, coaching,
> mentorship, mastermind, etcetera.

Logically, you may know that all expenses are not created equal.

Emotionally, how you feel about expenses may not match your logical understanding.

This can be a blind spot and could be creating resistance in your business growth.

> *"Constant struggle is a function of fear. Inner peace is a function of self-love."*
>
> — AVADHI DHRUV

BELIEFS THAT ARE BLOCKING YOUR BUSINESS GROWTH

Receiver blocks will also show up as resistance to reach out for support Watch out for this.

Referring to the story about the drowning man, this is a classic example of a receiver block, which is the internal resistance to asking for, allowing, and receiving help.

In business, and in life, it is extremely important to receive as it is to give.

As the book *The Go-Giver* explains so beautifully, giving and receiving is like exhaling and inhaling. In order to breathe freely, you have to both exhale and inhale fully.

If you only exhale, and refuse to inhale, you would be stuck. If you only inhale, and refuse to exhale, again you would be stuck.

It is only when you recognize that exhaling and inhaling are both equally important, and neither is better or worse than the other, that you can breathe freely and enjoy your life fully.

In a similar way, you are often brought up believing that either giving is important and receiving is bad, or that receiving is good and giving is not much of an option for you because you are not good enough or don't have enough to give.

No matter what the case may be with your upbringing, realize that giving and receiving are both equally important to have a healthy balance in life and business. Neither is better or worse than the other, they are just two sides of the same coin.

When you realize this, you can open up more, and be free to give and receive without constraints, feelings of scarcity, or any kind of guilt.

Remember, the more you give, the more you will receive. And the more you are able to receive, the more you will develop your capacity to give. This is the law of Karma – Action and Reaction, Giving and Receiving. Improve your muscle for receiving, so that you can create abundant value and share it with the world through your business.

You learn various behaviors and pick up thoughts from your parents, family, society, school, and people around when you are a young child, and sometimes, what you learned early on turns into limiting thoughts and behaviors in your adult life which keep you from moving forward and achieving the dreams you wish to achieve.

Most of these limiting thoughts, behaviors, and habitual patterns exist as beliefs and perceptions stored in your subconscious mind. Since they are in the mind below the surface of your awareness, you are often not consciously aware of these. Nonetheless, they do their part in keeping you stuck and hold you back from taking the right actions for your business success.

For example, I had always unconsciously put an income ceiling on myself that I cannot earn more money than my husband because I had it ingrained in my subconscious mind that it would inevitably cause problems in my marriage. I also had inherited that I should not earn more money than other family members because I had believed that it would somehow be seen as being disrespectful and I would be treated with contempt as a result. Such fears kept me playing small and trying to stay safe, which evidently kept my income low, until I recognized these beliefs that blocked my growth, and I chose to shift my beliefs in mind to free me up. I removed my income ceiling because I decided I don't want to have any ceiling at all. Any number of unconscious beliefs and programs like these could be holding you back from your growth in terms of your business income and your personality.

In all of my sessions with my clients, I help them become aware of any limiting patterns that may be keeping them stuck, and then I leverage some powerful tools to shift those programs from being limiting to transforming into empowering beliefs that help my clients move forward toward their business dreams.

First step in this process is to recognize whether something unconsciously is stopping you from taking an action that would otherwise make sense for you to make growth in your business.

Second step is to identify the exact limiting belief, and state it in one sentence. For example, I am not capable of handling more money.

Third step is to create what you would like to believe instead, which would be more empowering for you. For example, I am capable and have the knowledge to handle large amounts of money. This newly created empowering belief can be anything that is most emotionally meaningful to you.

Fourth and final step is to create conscious and subconscious alignment with superconscious permission and ensure that the older limiting belief gets replaced with this new empowering belief you just created.

The above is a simplified version of the process for the purposes of this book, however, I go through the process with a deep level of care and more thorough inspection, during my client sessions, to ensure I completely capture the exact limiting belief and transform it into an empowering belief for you to move forward in your business.

As you grow as an entrepreneur, you will need to recognize that business is not a solo sport. It is a team sport. Building the right team for your business is as critical to its success as having the right mindset to begin with. Therefore, knowing this from the start can help you create your plans in the right direction, and not knowing this can cause you a lot of unnecessary stress.

It takes a healthy balance of giving and receiving muscle to be able to create a productive, high-performing team in business. Keep in mind, the more you will understand and accept yourself, the more you will be equipped to be a great leader and have a wonderful team to lead as you progress in your entrepreneurial journey.

PITFALLS OF BUSINESS SUCCESS AND FAILURE

Pitfalls of business success – if success turns into arrogance, success can be short lived. It is important to have a guide who can spot this self-sabotage and show you when you need to give credit for success to your clients and team members, and stay grounded in your humility.

Pitfalls of failure – if you had attachment to particular outcomes in your business goals, and those did not materialize, this might be a major disappointment and can crush your self-confidence and damage your self-image.

Always remember, that failure is never a person; it's only an incident.

It is important to debrief every incident by asking the four questions (what worked, what did not work, what did I learn, and what did I learn about myself) so you can gather valuable insights and wisdom from that experience, release the emotional charge from that situation, and move forward with being whole and complete within yourself.

You can do this by yourself, or work with an experienced guide who can help you with this so your self-confidence can be boosted from every incident of so-called "failure." This way, every failure can become a blessing in disguise, and you get to be a true alchemist in your life and business journey ahead.

FOUR SIGNS IT'S TIME TO HIRE A SPIRITUAL BUSINESS COACH

You had a life-long dream of being an entrepreneur and owning your business.

You wanted to pursue your passions and true purpose in life to make a difference in the world.

You finally did it. After all the doubt, fear, and challenges, you have your business.

First of all, let's pause to acknowledge this significant accomplishment.

Have you congratulated yourself? Let's do it now.

Okay, so now you're thinking, "I still feel those nagging feelings of doubt and fear now with even more challenges than before."

Are you having any of the following thoughts on a regular basis?

- I feel afraid of being seen for who I am. I'm afraid I don't matter.
- I need more training and certifications to prove my worth.
- Will I ever have the lifestyle and freedom that I desire?
- I have a lot of ideas, but don't know what to focus on first. I feel overwhelmed and confused about my priorities.
- And so on.

These thoughts, and the feelings they trigger can consume you, and significantly deter you from your path to success. If you are having these thoughts, it may be the right time for you to work with a spiritual business coach.

Here are the four signs it may be time to hire a spiritual business coach.

1. You Feel Afraid of Being Seen

Are you afraid, feel vulnerable and unsafe while being visible to other people? Well, you may just have a classic case of the fear of being seen.

2. You Lack Confidence in Yourself and/ or Your Business

Do you secretly doubt your ability to succeed as an entrepreneur? Do you feel like your product or service may not have enough value? These are signs that you could benefit from a boost in the self-worth and confidence departments.

3. You Are Trying to Create Work-Life Balance

A lot of entrepreneurs feel stuck in an endless loop of working harder, not smarter. It may have gotten ingrained in you that you need to work those "extra hours" in order to pull this off. This is where you may be missing out on personal or family time.

4. You Feel Overwhelmed and Confused about Your Business

If you are being honest with yourself, you don't know what one thing you should focus on next to achieve the success that you desire.

If you resonate with any or all of the above, you are in the right place, right here right now, reading this.

A spiritual business coach helps entrepreneurs and business leaders reconnect with their inner genius.

By working with a spiritual business coach, you can achieve the following outcomes, and more.

1. Show up confidently in the world as your true, authentic self.
2. Feel proud of yourself and know you are admired by the people in your life.
3. Create freedom to live your ideal lifestyle.
4. Feel empowered to create massive income in your business, while pursuing your true passion and purpose.
5. Have clarity about the exact priorities to focus on in your business to create the next level of success.

You can keep going at it on your own, or you can give yourself the gift of an experienced guide to support you in your entrepreneurial journey. This step alone can be a huge breakthrough for you in enhancing self-worth and confidence for yourself and your business.

Ready to reclaim the power in your business? I recommend you look for a spiritual business coach you can trust.

> *"When you learn to receive, you can truly give huge value and create a life of abundance."*
>
> — AVADHI DHRUV

12

TRANSFORM THE WORLD THROUGH YOUR BUSINESS

You have come a long way.

At this point, you have gained important clarity about the problems you currently face, and why they are worth solving in order to achieve the business success you desire. You have learned the importance of applying the Karma Yog principle to your life to create an actionable Abundance Path for yourself moving forward.

You have established the direction that you will move your business forward through your three- to five-year vision, key intentions for the current year, and top three goals.

You also know the steps for boosting your self-confidence by connecting with your intuition, understanding your purpose, aligning with your market and dream client, and leveraging your unique zone of genius.

You are now free to show up fully and be seen in your entrepreneurial journey. You are more connected to your purpose, your Dharma, than you have ever been.

You have also become more aware of what fears

could come up to block or deter your progress. You understand that you can transcend any fears of success, and are ready to chase those breakthroughs to ensure continuous growth and expansion for your business.

You also know the true way to honor and love yourself, which is to detach from any external expectations or outcomes. This will aid you in providing the most authentic value to the world.

You're aware of any further obstacles that could come up in your way, so you can best be equipped to handle and overcome them.

You understand the importance of having a long-term strategic plan that will support sustainable growth for you and your business.

Most importantly, you are energized and excited to create the dream income, impact, and lifestyle you desire through your business!

LOOKING FOR MORE SUPPORT IN YOUR BUSINESS GROWTH?

If you need support, reach out, and I can hold your hand through the entire process step by step.

PATIENCE AND PERSISTENCE

Patience and persistence are key to winning in the end. As long as you don't give up on your dreams or give in to life's circumstances and tests, you keep persevering through the challenges that come up, you will achieve the success that you so deserve.

What comes first: happiness or success?

This might sound like the chicken and the egg question.

I think the answer may depend on how you define happiness and success.

Happiness, defined as an internal state of being, which can be felt as a pleasant, calm, peaceful, joyful feeling, is then part of your inner world.

Success, defined as abundant wealth, prosperity in lifestyle, and freedom of time and choice, is then part of your outer world.

Your inner world consists of your beliefs, perceptions, thoughts, and feelings.

Your outer world consists of the tangible results you see and have around you.

So, what comes first: happiness or success?

It's similar to asking, what manifests first: your inner world or your outer world?

There's no doubt that when something desirable happens in your outer world, you may feel happiness in your inner world. In that sense, you could say that success comes before happiness.

However, have you ever met someone or heard of people who are successful in their outer world and still not happy in their inner world? I know I have. I've also seen people who are just happy, and don't have any outer world success to connect their happiness to.

So, perhaps, it's not true that outer world success always comes before inner world happiness. Then, can inner world happiness come before outer world success?

This is where the water gets deep, so stick with me, I'll be your float.

The universal truth is that inner world happiness always comes before outer world success, by law. This is because it's your inner world that creates your outer world.

In fact, happiness always leads to success, and unhappiness leads to struggle and failure. This is good news, right? Now, you don't need to be unhappy all the time to have success. You are free to be happy before you create success.

So, if you want to have success in the outer world, it's important to know that the happiness in your inner world needs to come first.

Look for ways to create happiness in your inner world- in your beliefs, perceptions, thoughts, and feelings. Happy beliefs are empowering beliefs. Happy perceptions are loving perceptions. Happy thoughts are powerful thoughts. Happy feelings are, well, happy feelings.

Your happy inner world will guarantee your outer world success, every time, hands down.

"Patience is not the act of waiting. Rather, it is an awareness that gifts us the willingness to wait."

— AVADHI DHRUV

Patience is often misunderstood to be the act of waiting for a long, long time.

It is misunderstood to be a verb, as if it were something that needs to be done. In this context, when someone says, "have patience," you interpret it as "just wait (with no end in sight)," so you think it calls for inaction, and that leaves you feeling powerless and disempowered.

It can lead to hopelessness, lack of clarity, and frustration.

In this case, the real tragedy is that you completely miss out on the magic that patience has, inherently, in it.

First, you will need to understand what patience is not, and what it is.

Patience is not a verb; it is a noun. It is defined as an ability to accept or endure. This definition may be difficult to understand and apply in your day-to-day life.

So, in more practical terms, you must understand that patience is not the act of waiting. Rather, it is an awareness that gifts you the willingness to wait.

Patience is not about doing or not doing something. Rather, it is a state of being.

It is a powerful state of being, which arises from faith. Faith is an inner knowing, that everything in life is unfolding in perfect order, for your highest good.

Infinite patience, therefore, is an awareness that gifts you the willingness to wait, for eternity.

Beware, the willingness to wait for eternity, does not mean there is a compulsion or obligation to wait forever. It also doesn't mean that you will "have to" wait for a long, long time. The compulsion, obligation, and "have to" are all in the world of impatience.

Impatience comes from having attachment to an outcome which you believe will make you happy at some point in the future. Impatience automatically means that you are not happy in the present moment.

Impatience also means that you believe happiness will come from something or someone outside of yourself. Impatience means that happiness is not a choice you currently have, rather that happiness is an elusive commodity that you have to chase after, in order to achieve it.

In truth, happiness is not a commodity to be chased after. Just like patience, happiness is also a state of being.

The beautiful truth about any state of being is that it can exist only in the present moment, and that it is a choice you have which you can powerfully make from within yourself.

You can choose patience from within yourself. You can choose happiness from within yourself. Both patience and happiness are states of being that can exist for you in the present moment.

Now here is the magical part about all of this. When you choose powerful states of being, like patience and happiness, you create yourself into a magnet for miracles in life. You create your electromagnetic energy field around you, which attracts exactly what you focus on with your intention, into your life and circumstances.

So, this is how choosing patience can help you create the life of your dreams.

This is why, patience is a virtue, and infinite patience, is the foundation for manifesting miracles in your life.

"Happiness is at the source of success, not at odds with it. True happiness leads to success, not the other way around."

— AVADHI DHRUV

THE PRICE TO PAY AND OPPORTUNITY COST OF WAITING

The price to pay for a life of abundance and fulfillment is great because the reward is great as well – it is the ultimate gift in life.

Life will throw huge tests your way in this journey.

For best results and the highest chance of success, take the hand of an experienced guide, and place your faith in someone you can trust. You will have a much better and a richer experience overall. You will also be able to create faster results as far as achieving your goals are concerned.

The opportunity cost of waiting and struggling alone for too long is that ultimately you would give up on your dreams. You may buy into the falsehood that your dream life is not possible, or that it is "unrealistic," which is furthest from the truth.

Taking the right actions, reaching out for support, and building a team, are crucial steps for you to stay in the game of entrepreneurship.

Don't give up on your dreams; the world needs your light so that Heaven on Earth can be created. You were born with a purpose which is the piece of the puzzle the world is waiting for.

You can either spend your time and energy to keep going on your own, or invest money to save you time and energy for accelerated growth with a positive return for your business. The choice is yours. Choose wisely.

> *"Change is the name of the game. Choose to focus now on creating a change for the betterment of the future."*

— AVADHI DHRUV

CLIENT RESULTS

My clients get crystal clear on their "why" for being in business.

They get truly connected to their purpose, their passion, and inner power, which makes them unstoppable in the face of any circumstance.

As a result of this unwavering confidence, they take inspired actions, and their business grows and flourishes.

They naturally have increased income in terms of revenue.

They are strategic about their business growth and pay attention to their finances, so their business is profitable.

My clients do what they love and make an impact in the world through their genius.

They show up fully and create a lifestyle of true freedom for themselves.

Does this sound like something you're interested in for yourself?

This level of authenticity and awareness isn't something that happens overnight.

It isn't a temporary change. It is a complete transformation.

I'm interested in working with people who are committed to their purpose, their mission in life, and take their business seriously because it's not just a side gig for them. It's their entire life's work.

Do you see yourself as being one of these people who is hungry for transformation and growth?

If so, your dream life is awaiting you.

Alan was extremely frustrated with the entire state of his business and what he seemed to have "inherited" was a mountain of problems and heaps of constraints that he did not know how to navigate through.

Profits were down, revenues were low, and stress was high. Hopes were completely non-existent as fear and insecurity prevailed. This created a toxic atmosphere in the entire team, and affected his family in terms of health, wealth, and happiness.

When all areas of his life were at risk, he reached out for help in a discreet way.

On the first day, we captured all of the millions of thoughts he had running around in his mind and painted a concise picture of the current state, as he saw it. When he saw those in front of his eyes, he felt a sense of being heard and seen in a way he hadn't been before. He felt safe in that space I created for him. Suddenly, insecurity and fear calmed down and his system started shifting gears. We then explored what his dreams were, hopes were, and possibly touched on his goals briefly. It was too early to talk about specifics of goals. However, we were able to capture the gist of his desires and how he wanted to be able to feel about his business and while working in it for growth. We identified that his desire was of joy, fun, excitement, freedom, and adventure. So, we called it, the Journey to Bliss.

As far from bliss as the state of his business was at the time we started, in every session we uncovered new ways of thinking that could create new possibilities. We addressed various areas of business, like the beliefs and perceptions of the current and past team, the state of cash flow and finances, the logistics of inventory and operations, the communications with customers for boosting sales, making pricing decisions, and strategic ways to negotiate deals. We inquired into the inner state of mind about what money is. We created a way in which all team members could build mutual trust and respect to win as a powerful team. We cultivated the mantra of "Together we rise, together we learn and grow."

His commitment to transformation was big enough to allow the complete shift to happen, from the inside and out. He has come a long way to having peace of mind and clarity, hopefulness, and even excitement for the next chapter of his business' growth. He has adopted new ways of thinking and his team has become powerful and more supportive for sustaining the business success. Cash flow and finances have become more fluid and sales have increased. The business is well on its way to be sustainably profitable, and foundationally strong to be able to weather any storms that may come along the way. The biggest difference is in the peaceful night of sleep that Alan can now enjoy because in his heart he is content, and grateful to be alive.

If Alan's life can change by being open to this level of transformation in his business, so can yours. All you need to do is step up and claim what is rightfully yours, your dream life and destiny.

MY WISH FOR YOU

My wish for you is that you choose your dreams above all obstacles life may throw at you and live your life purposefully through your business. If you have questions, reach out to my team; we are here to help.

Love thyself. Love yourself. What does this mean? Don't you hear this often? It is possibly the most misunderstood concept in our world today, so you must have clarity on this. Love yourself means love your inner self. Love your spirit which is your true nature, your soul. Honor your strengths, your talents, your abilities, your gifts which have come to you naturally. Be present with your nature from within. Your inner awareness, which is infinite, is within you and all around you. Connect with the life force that loves you unconditionally and gives you life. Love that life force!

Honor that life force as it honors you. When you are in harmony with your life force, it will show you how powerful you are and why you are here on this Earth, in this life, what is your calling, your true purpose in your life. It all starts with truly honoring and loving thyself, thy soul.

Who I am for the readers is a soul who simply loves life. What inspired me is seeing the potential in humans all over the world which remains untapped because they simply don't love their true selves.

The message for you is simply to love thyself to know your true self and love thy soul. Why, you ask? So that you can live full and die empty. Why, you ask again? Why not? I ask you. What else is there if not the fulfillment of the purpose of your life? What else is there if not a life full of grace, love and joy. All that you seek is within your heart; only you can allow your soul to guide you through toward abundance and fulfillment. It all starts with loving yourself.

As you finish this book, I have a dream for you. Will you allow me a moment to stand for your greatness?

My dream for you is to emerge from reading this book as a newly empowered being. You are now ready to pursue your dreams of a worthy life unique to your heart's desires.

Maybe you wish to start that business you have always had in the back of your mind. Maybe you have a fresh, new business idea that came from discovering your true purpose. Maybe you want to reclaim the power in your existing business. Or, maybe, you don't have it exactly figured out yet, but you are inspired to move forward.

In any case, I know that you are a powerful being connected to an infinite Source. As you connect deeper with your intuition, you will be able to create the heart-centered, impactful, aligned, and prosperous business you desire.

I am confident in your abilities as an entrepreneur. I also know that the biggest risk in business comes from trying to do it all alone. No business owner has ever prospered by doing it all alone. That is just not how business works.

Whether you wish to apply for my coaching services, or look for other resources, you will need help to grow your business. Having a coach or mentor to guide you and hold you accountable while helping you create your powerful business strategy is key for your long-term business success.

"Love is the unconditional power of trust and confidence that emanates from the heart."

— AVADHI DHRUV

READY TO TAKE THE NEXT STEP FOR YOUR DREAM BUSINESS?

You now know what it takes to become a self-realized being, reconnect with your true self, and love yourself fully. My clients and I have leveraged this understanding to create a bigger impact on this planet through businesses that align with our unique purposes.

Now, it is your time to shine your light.

When you are ready to make a profound impact through your unique genius in the world, schedule your 1:1 call with me at https://www.avadhi.guru/ to get started.

"Love is the true and authentic language of the Divine."

— AVADHI DHRUV

WHAT IS THE GREATEST REWARD OF ENTREPRENEURSHIP?

There is a secret that only the most successful entrepreneurs know.

The greatest reward of entrepreneurship is way beyond the income you can make in terms of money. It is even beyond the freedom you can have in lifestyle through it. It is also beyond the impact you can create in the world. It is about the person you become through it. The confidence and wisdom gained from your experiences as an entrepreneur can never be lost or taken away from you. This becomes your invaluable treasure that you will have with you forever and ever.

Who you become is the most valuable reward you get by persevering through to success with your entrepreneurial spirit.

> *"The moment you start living with a sense of purpose in your current life, you will start experiencing fulfillment."*
>
> — AVADHI DHRUV

WHY I WROTE THIS BOOK

I wrote this book because I saw a lot of misery in the world. I was born in India and as I grew up, I saw a lot of poverty around me which shook me to the core. I felt like I had been called to create bliss for all those people in the world who were suffering. I am aware that suffering is optional in life, and I felt like a lot of pain and suffering had to do with scarcity.

I thought about how I could create an abundance of resources for all the people in the world. This question kept ruminating in my mind. I thought that if I could find a way to create abundance in the world, that would solve the problem of scarcity which people seemed to be experiencing.

Now, on the other hand, I saw that a lot of people who were living in an abundance of resources, were not truly satisfied and happy. They didn't experience true freedom in their lives. That brought on the question of, "Why are people who have money and an abundance of resources still not happy?" The answer to that, I found, was in the lack of fulfillment. I found that when inner fulfillment is missing from people's lives, they are unable to be truly happy.

This brought me to the realization that the combination of abundance and fulfillment can create true happiness for people. This unique combination can be the definition for true success.

I also came to the conclusion that only true success can create real freedom for people in their lives, and when people live their lives fully, the world would become Heaven on Earth!

So, here's why I wrote this book. This book is truly inspired by my awareness of my mission on Earth in this life. I have realized that my life has been divinely designed to bring about the mission of creating Heaven on Earth through entrepreneurship.

Now, why through entrepreneurship? This is based on another realization I had when I was contemplating on what is the best way to bring abundance and fulfillment to all the people in the world.

When I thought about this question, what came to me is that in order to create abundance, the world would need to have lots of products and services that help people by making their lives easier, happier, healthier, and more convenient. Also, human beings created money, which is a measure and a medium of exchanging value. So, abundance has to do with the flow of money, the circulation of currency, and the exchange of value amongst all of humanity. How fast and how well that flow continues is what creates an upward spiral of momentum and growth for humanity.

The best system I found that could create this upward spiral of momentum through products and services and exchange of value for humans is a business. As I explain it, a business is a system of systems, and every entrepreneur is like a spider who can create this system of systems like an intricately designed spider web. Just as every spider's web is unique to the spider who created it, every business is unique to the entrepreneur who built the system.

I realized that the best way to bring abundance to the world was to empower people to be entrepreneurs. The beautiful truth is that all humans are naturally born with entrepreneurial skills, and have abilities to think creatively and solve problems. By empowering that inborn ability within people, the world could become a better place. By enabling natural creative problem solvers in the world to spot problems and solve them in unique ways, more resources could be brought to the world in sustainable ways. Just as spiders, entrepreneurs would create a unique spider web, also known as their business, and then create solutions in terms of products and services to offer people in the world.

As entrepreneurs contribute and create abundance for the world, they would also receive money in return. Ultimately, solving problems through their business would create abundance for the entrepreneur themselves, and this would help them have freedom in their lifestyle and create an ideal life for themselves. This creates a win-win situation.

The above solves the first part of the equation which

was about abundance. Next, the second part of the equation, which is equally important, is about fulfillment.

I pondered over the question of how to create fulfillment for entrepreneurs so they can experience freedom and happiness in the process of creating their unique spider web.

When I thought of a spider, I noticed that not a single spider creates a spider web while being miserable doing it. There seems to be an innate sense of peace, contentment, satisfaction, and even happiness while nature creates anything in the world. So how would it make sense if a human being created their business in a state of scarcity, lack, fear, frustration, and all sorts of misery?

I realized that it is necessary, and extremely important that an entrepreneur be in a state of flow, peace, love, and gratitude, while creating their unique business. So, how does an entrepreneur stay in a consistent state of flow and creation? This could be possible if the entrepreneur stays connected to an infinite source of flow and creation.

So now, where can the entrepreneur find such a source? This is the zillion-dollar question! Now, I have found that source, and it isn't as far as you might think. The journey to connect with it isn't as long as you might imagine. The truth is that this source already exists within each entrepreneur. Perhaps that is surprising, and yet it is the ultimate truth that I have found in my journey as an entrepreneur.

So, there you have it. This is why I wrote this book. It is to inspire every human on the planet to connect with their source within. It is to encourage humans to tap into their entrepreneurial abilities so that they can naturally create a life of abundance and fulfillment for themselves and for the world through their businesses. It is, ultimately, so that humans can live on this planet and have an experience of being in Heaven on Earth!

APPENDIX A: AFFIRMATIONS

Affirmations for speaking wealth into existence: Repeat these affirmations every day for at least one week, and observe the changes you feel by doing this exercise.

"I have a large, steady, dependable, permanent financial income now. Every day in every way I am growing more and more financially prosperous now."

"I give thanks for a quick and substantial increase in my financial income now."

"Everything and everybody prospers me now, and I prosper everything and everybody now."

"I now work financial wonders in my life with prosperity declarations."

"My words are charged with prospering power."

"I praise my world now; I praise my financial affairs now. All the wealth that has not come to me in the past is manifesting riches for me now."

"Words of praise prosper me now."

"Things are getting better for me financially; my income will increase."

APPENDIX B: BELIEF STATEMENTS

Use the statements below, or create your own empowering Belief Statements, to plant seeds of abundance, prosperity, success, and peace in your life.

Choose at least five statements from the list below (unless you have created your own, in which case you can use those), and start using them today. This is a way you can fuel your mind with positive and self-loving thoughts.

Repeat your chosen belief statements every day for at least one week and observe the changes you feel by doing this exercise.

- I expect and receive miracles.
- What I focus on expands.
- I am a divine being with a divine purpose.
- I have important gifts to share in the world.
- I am guided by infinite intelligence.
- I am a money magnet.
- I can handle any challenge when and if it arises.
- There is more than enough for everyone.

APPENDIX B: BELIEF STATEMENTS

- My thoughts become things.
- I take successful baby steps.
- I'm always moving forward.
- I make the right decision.
- I bless that which I want.
- The more people I serve, the richer I am.
- The more solutions I create, the richer I am.
- I can do anything.
- My word is law in the Universe.
- I am the eye of the storm.
- I love my life.
- I succeed with grace, elegance, and ease.
- I earn money when I sleep, when I play, and even when I am on vacation.
- I am a teacher. I have important information to share.
- I acknowledge and celebrate my successes.
- I manifest the glory of God that is within me.
- I am powerful beyond measure.
- My highest desires are manifesting now.
- I follow my heart. My heart has only answers.
- I see all changes being in my highest interest.
- I am curious about all that is happening in my life.
- I stay in the present, here and now.
- The quality of my life is equal to the quality of my rituals.
- I take massive action.
- I am decisive.
- I think big.
- I am excellent at managing my energy.
- People around me are intelligent, confident, energetic, powerful, efficient, and motivated.

ACKNOWLEDGMENTS

Five years ago, an idea for my first book was planted in my mind from the heart of the Divine. I am grateful to Source for planting the seed of sacred purpose in my being.

As Newton once wrote, "If I have seen further, it is by standing on the shoulders of giants."

This quote applies perfectly in the case of this book. It is only with the blessings and support of the beautiful souls mentioned below that this book has been able to be born into existence.

First and foremost, I thank my parents for nurturing my innocence and inner genius with unconditional love every step of the way. Mom, you are like the gardener who always saw infinite potential in me, and Dad, you are the shelter that cultivated my growth no matter what came my way. I am eternally grateful for you both, and I love you both to infinity.

I thank my grandparents and entire extended family for believing in my potential to be unlimited, for nourishing my genius with the strongest values, and for providing me with a powerful foundation to speak from. A special thanks to my paternal and maternal grandfathers, for being my role models of entrepreneurs who have stood for a better future for our family, the community, and the world. To my brothers, Urnil and Tanooj, thank you for always having my back. I love you both more than you can imagine! Thank you, to my sister, Anuja, for the encouragement you provided in my initial stages of the book journey.

I feel blessed to have Guruji Shri Rishi Prabhakarji as my role model and guide in becoming a world leader as an entrepreneur. I have learned to dream big, live a life of abundance and true freedom, and the value of contribution from the great examples of so many gurus in India, including my Guruji.

I thank all the teachers in my childhood who have inculcated devotion and imbibed values in my character that make me the person I am today. I am grateful to my school, Rishi Vidyalaya Gurukulam, for the generous contribution it has made toward all of us children. The days in the residential school are some of my best memories in life.

I thank all my instructors, including my Psych-K® instructor, Karen McKy, and my coaches over the years, for bringing out the best in me and shaping me into being a responsible human being for the betterment of humanity and the world.

A humble thanks to all my friends through school, college, and beyond, for sharing my journey and accepting me for who I am. Thanks, Elle, for cheering me on in my entrepreneurial adventure and for my book dreams!

A very special thanks to Dr. Angela Lauria and the Author Incubator team – Madeline; Ramses; Lisa; Jasmine; Karmi; my incredible managing editor, Cory; my amazing designer, Jennifer; and brilliant proofreader, Natasa.

Angela came into my life truly as an angel with the

specific purpose of birthing this book into the world. Thank you, Angela, for putting the right constraints around my creativity and lovingly nourishing this book till its birth in 3D, in service to humanity.

Thank you, Cory, for making my book journey seamless, and for being a beam of joy throughout the editorial process of this book. You have coached me through ever so gently that I feel like I have been genuinely supported. Thank you for carrying me through all of the fears and doubts, to the other side into a beautiful land of confidence, clarity, and completion of the book. You have made me feel like an excellent storyteller and an accomplished writer. Thank you for all you do for us, your authors.

Thank you once again, the entire TAI team, for being the co-manifestors and executors of this book project. A loving thanks to my fellow authors for sharing a beautiful space with me in the group. The incubator that Angela, the team, and you all created together was exactly what I needed to become a first time ever published author.

I thank my team members – Kelly, Anisa, Michelle, and Amanda – for being my rocks, cheerleaders, companions, and loving facilitators of the entire journey from conception to reality. Kelly, thank you for your tremendous contribution from the inception to the organizational support for this book. I appreciate your passion and hours of focused attention that went into creating this book's content to be as beautiful as it could be. Anisa, thank you for your patient and encouraging presence that helped in moving this project forward. You are a kind soul, and I appreciate you for that. Michelle, thank you for sharing your experience and supportive feedback which gave this project great momentum, and gave me the freedom to be true to myself. You bring a cheerful and positive energy to our team and I truly value you for that. Amanda, thank you for being a steward for the book project to reach completion and beyond. Your compassion for the entrepreneurs we serve is exemplary, and I look forward to growing our impact further ahead.

A shout out to all my previous team members, colleagues, and countless more souls who have helped me directly and indirectly in being able to focus on this book project. You know who you are. Your presence in my life has contributed toward the completion of this book, and I'm grateful to you for that.

Finally, I am beyond grateful to my husband, Chirag. You have been my pillar of strength through my entire entrepreneurial journey, and I am incredibly proud of who we have grown to become over the years. Thank you for being my guiding light on the darkest days, and for sharing this book journey with me. You have been with me in all the moments when I needed you the most. Thank you for believing in me, being my confidant, and understanding me deeply in the most sensitive stages of this process. You are a patient and fun-loving partner to have, and I adore you with all my heart.

Laying on a sandy beach under the open sky, witnessing the vastness of the ocean, there is a place where I find myself. As a tiny little bit of existence, so insignificant and yet present on this planet Earth, it makes me wonder, why am I here? What is the reason for me being alive?!

It is then that Source whispers in my ears, that when such massive forces of nature are working their magic, so can I. They are a manifestation of the divine, and so am I.

It is the divinity that wants to manifest itself through you, in all its glory, so who are you to stop that abundant flow? Let it glow. Full of light, let it shine. Be yourself, and be Divine.

To you, my reader, thank you for being you.

ABOUT THE AUTHOR

Avadhi Dhruv is a spiritual business coach and author who helps entrepreneurs and business leaders reconnect with their magnificence. She helps heart-centered entrepreneurs reclaim the power in their businesses so they can create financial abundance and inner fulfillment, while making a positive impact in the world.

After having a successful corporate career in engineering and management, Avadhi still felt the urge to explore her higher purpose in life. In 2014, she decided to embark on an entrepreneurial journey to connect with her inner genius and uncover the best way in which she was meant to serve the world.

After investing significant amounts of time, money, and energy into her personal development by completing numerous courses, consuming countless books and videos, participating in top-tier business training events and workshops, hiring and working with coaches, and doing a lot of soul searching, Avadhi experienced tremendous growth and realized that her passion and purpose in life is to make a positive impact in the world through empowering other entrepreneurs in their businesses.

Avadhi founded the brand, Avadhi.guru™, with the intention of bringing a holistic approach to businesses. She finds fulfillment in helping entrepreneurs gain clarity and confidence in achieving their business dreams. Through her books and programs, she helps her clients create and execute on strategic plans for their businesses, where they have unlimited potential for growth in income, freedom in lifestyle, and a deep understanding of their worth as a business owner.

Today, Avadhi is a thought leader and world leader whose vision is to create a world of abundance and fulfillment by empowering heart-centered, conscious entrepreneurs to take their businesses to new heights. Her clients have included budding entrepreneurs to leaders of multi-million dollar international businesses who have successfully made transformational changes in their businesses and lives.

Avadhi is the Chief Transformation Officer at Prabhat – a global brand and more than fifty years strong family-owned business. In a few short years, she has helped the Prabhat group of companies achieve multi-levels of top-line and bottom-line growth along with the ability to thrive in any kind of economic climate. Avadhi is a Psych-K® Facilitator and uses her skills and experience coupled with powerful transformational tools to help her clients create long-lasting business results.

Avadhi was born in India and has been connected to spirituality since her earliest years. Her parents practiced meditation, yoga, breathwork, and took her with them to various retreats in nature as a young child. Avadhi attended a residential school in India, a Gurukulam, which provided an environment of holistic education interwoven with spiritual practices. At her school, the focus was on developing children into entrepreneurial-minded world leaders who have the humility of a saint, the knowledge of a teacher, and the wisdom of a guru. Her unique upbringing has been a major propellant in her accelerated development in terms of knowledge and wisdom beyond her biological years.

Avadhi moved from India to the United States with her parents in her high school years, and thereafter, attended Georgia Institute of Technology for her undergrad in Industrial and Systems Engineering. After graduating with honors in May 2011 as part of her corporate career, she moved to sunny San Diego, California, which is where she currently resides.

Avadhi is passionate about personal development and is a lifelong learner. She loves supporting her amazing family, spending time in nature, and remaining present throughout her day.

Avadhi is grateful for every step of her journey so far which has led her to being her true expression as a coach, author, and guru. She believes that every human has entrepreneurial potential, and every entrepreneur has an Inner Genius that deserves to be expressed so that business owners can have an abundant and fulfilling life.

For more information about Avadhi, visit:
www.avadhi.guru/about-avadhi.

ABOUT DIFFERENCE PRESS

Difference Press is the publishing arm of The Author Incubator, an Inc. 500 award-winning company that helps business owners and executives grow their brand, establish thought leadership, and get customers, clients, and highly-paid speaking opportunities, through writing and publishing books.

While traditional publishers require that you already have a large following to guarantee they make money from sales to your existing list, our approach is focused on using a book to grow your following – even if you currently don't have a following. This is why we charge an up-front fee but never take a percentage of revenue you earn from your book.

☞ MORE THAN A COACH. MORE THAN A PUBLISHER. ✍

We work intimately and personally with each of our authors to develop a revenue-generating strategy for the book. By using a Lean Startup style methodology, we guarantee the book's success before we even start writing. We provide all the technical support authors need with editing, design, marketing, and publishing, the emotional support you would get from a book coach to help you manage anxiety and time constraints, and we serve as a strategic thought partner engineering the book for success.

The Author Incubator has helped almost 2,000 entrepreneurs write, publish, and promote their non-fiction books. Our authors have used their books to gain international media exposure, build a brand and marketing following, get lucrative speaking engagements, raise awareness of their product or service, and attract clients and customers.

☞ ARE YOU READY TO WRITE A BOOK? ✍

As a client, we will work with you to make sure your book gets done right and that it gets done quickly. The Author Incubator provides one-stop for strategic book consultation, author coaching to manage writer's block and anxiety, full-service professional editing, design, and self-publishing services, and book marketing and launch campaigns. We sell this as one package so our clients are not slowed down with contradictory advice. We have a 99 percent success rate with nearly all of our clients completing their books, publishing them, and reaching bestseller status upon launch.

☞ APPLY NOW AND BE OUR NEXT SUCCESS STORY ✍

To find out if there is a significant ROI for you to write a book, get on our calendar by completing an application at www.TheAuthorIncubator.com/apply.

OTHER BOOKS BY DIFFERENCE PRESS

The Scholarship Playbook for Parents of Student-Athletes: Stop Fouling Out and Start Scoring Money for College by Dr. Simoné Edwards

Longevity: Reinvent Yourself at Any Age by Maria L. Ellis, MBA

Leadership Parenting: Empower Your Child's Social Success by Mother Gopi Gita

Embracing Equity: Best Practices for Developing and Keeping a Winning Multi-Racial Leadership Team by Janine Hill, PhD

Weight Loss for High Achievers: Stop Self-Sabotage and Start Losing Weight by Karen King

When Marriage Needs a Miracle: The Modern Woman's Guide to Figure out the Future of Your Relationship by Shari Kubinec

The Speed of Passion: How Relationship-Based Leadership Drives Innovation by Carol Ann Langford

Profitable Online Programs: A Brief Guide to Creating and Launching an Impactful Digital Course, Then Scaling Your Biz with Your Own Expert Book! by Dr. Angela E. Lauria

Take Back Your Life: Find Hope and Freedom from Fibromyalgia Symptoms and Pain by Tami Stackelhouse

The $7-Trillion Shock Wave: 401K Investing Strategies with a Positive Impact in Our Shared Climate Future by Seann Stoner

Understanding the Profiles in Human Design: The Facilitator's Guide to Unleashing Potential by Robin Winn, MFT

GIFT FOR READERS

Thank you for reading!

I acknowledge you for giving yourself the time to absorb the wisdom shared in this book.

It is my wish that you achieve your highest potential in this life and fulfill your destiny while making a positive impact in the world.

It is important that you are empowered to embark on your entrepreneurial journey to create your dream business with unwavering confidence and clarity.

Looking for more wisdom and guidance for your entrepreneurial journey?

In order to support you further, I have created an exclusive playlist of Clear Intention Healing™ meditations you can use to create exponential growth in your income and in life.

In this exclusive playlist called "Healings and Guided Meditations," you will get immediate access to:

- Clear Intention Healing Meditation for Transmuting Anxiety, Stress, & Fear
- Success Manifestation Guided Meditation
- Clear Intention Healing Meditation for Setting Healthy Boundaries
- *... and SO much more!*

Email team@avadhi.guru to access the exclusive playlist of healing meditations I've created for you.

Also, if you haven't already, subscribe to my YouTube channel to receive regular insights on growing your income potential along with creating freedom in your lifestyle:
www.youtube.com/@AvadhiGuru

To get your copy of the companion workbook with fillable worksheets mentioned in the chapters of this book, visit this webpage: www.avadhi.guru/book

The entrepreneurs I work with have achieved the income growth and lifestyle freedom they desired, and you deserve to live your business dreams too! If you are ready to create a real income generating business you love, schedule your Abundance Call with me at
www.avadhi.guru/scheduling

Take the next step that intuitively feels right for you and unlock a whole new level of success that is in store for you!

OTHER BOOKS BY AVADHI

A Secret Guide to
Alchemize Conflict into Harmony,
Lead with Confidence, and Generate Profits

THE *Family* BUSINESS *Guru*

Avadhi Dhruv

www.ingramcontent.com/pod-product-compliance
Lightning Source LLC
Chambersburg PA
CBHW072155070526
44585CB00015B/1149